Staircase Design

Staircase Design

teNeues

Editor in chief: Paco Asensio

Editorial coordination: Haike Falkenberg

Original texts: Haike Falkenberg, Aurora Cuito (Types)

Art director: Mireia Casanovas Soley

Graphic design / Layout: Pilar Cano

English translation: Matthew Clarke

German translation: Inken Wolthaus

French translation: Michel Ficerai

Published by teNeues Publishing Group

teNeues Publishing Company
16 West 22nd Street, New York, NY 10010, USA
Tel.: 001-212-627-9090, Fax: 001-212-627-9511

teNeues Book Division
Kaistraße 18
40221 Düsseldorf, Germany
Tel.: 0049-(0)211-994597-0, Fax: 0049-(0)211-994597-40

teNeues Publishing UK Ltd.
P.O. Box 402
West Byfleet
KT14 7ZF, Great Britain
Tel.: 0044-1932-403509, Fax: 0044-1932-403514

teNeues France S.A.R.L.
4, rue de Valence, 75005 Paris, France
Tel.: 0033-1-55 76 62 05, Fax: 0033-1-55 76 64 19
www.teneues.com

ISBN: 3-8238-5572-7

Editorial project: © 2002 LOFT Publications
Via Laietana 32, 4º Of. 92
08003 Barcelona, Spain
Tel.: 0034 932 688 088
Fax: 0034 932 687 073
e-mail: loft@loftpublications.com
www.loftpublications.com

Printed by: Anman Gràfiques del Vallès, Spain
2005

Bibliographic information published by
Die Deutsche Bibliothek.
Die Deutsche Bibliothek lists this publication
in the Deutsche Nationalbibliografie;
detailed bibliographic data is available
in the Internet at http://dnb.ddb.de

Staircases

The staircase has existed since the dawn of time for one very specific purpose: to surmount gaps between different levels. For a long time staircases did nothing more than fulfil this aim and so their form was directly determined by their location, but new functions emerged as different civilizations evolved and the specific requirements of certain types of buildings started to influence the form of staircases.

These new functions were mainly the fruit of religious practices that associated staircases with mythological and philosophical concepts, so that, for example, the staircase became an expression of the ascension of the spirit. Even today, this symbolism can still be seen in the pyramids of ancient Egypt and the constructions of the Mayas and the Incas. Later on, secular architecture developed features intended to convey political and economic power and the staircase became a compositional element that acquired an increasing importance in the overall visual impact of many buildings.

However, the form of the staircase is not dependent on different historical styles – their influence barely extends beyond the decorative elements – but it does often embody a set of values or an aspiration towards technical perfection. These concepts became one of the driving forces behind the architectural and esthetic evolution of the staircase and gave rise to extraordinary works of art in every culture, without ever forsaking the staircase's primary purpose of connecting different levels. When it came to displaying status, the selection of materials was just as important as the function, as a staircase's cost or technical sophistication symbolized not only the wealth of the person responsible for its construction but also his social and intellectual standing.

As materials have continued to evolve, so, at the same time, the forms of staircases have changed. Clay and straw gave way to stone and now we have moved on to construction in steel and reinforced concrete. Advances in construction techniques played an increasingly important role as they opened up ever more audacious architectural possibilities. In this respect, the nineteenth century was hugely significant as it introduced extensive technical improvements. Steel and concrete made it possible to bridge considerable gaps while also adding safety features, as in the case of emergency exits resistant to fire. A more rational use of building materials – often used in combination – gave rise to a new formal diversity. Staircases lost their rigidity with the arrival of spiraled silhouettes, decorative forms and curves, but textures, lighting and the distribution of space all have a role to play as well. It could be said that the staircase has been dematerialized in order to preserve its basic character, its essential lines and its innate function – that of going up and down – although the imagination has sometimes managed to dream up impossible staircases, such as those of the Dutch artist M. C. Escher.

This book seeks to reveal the diversity of today's staircases and inspire readers to find or create their own ideal staircase. The form is the starting point for every staircase, so the book opens with an explanation of the most basic forms, illustrated with architectural drawings and photos. The next chapter is devoted to the presentation of the various materials used: stone, wood, reinforced concrete, metal, glass and combinations of these materials. Finally, there is an examination of details, such as banisters and steps, to highlight the elements that give a staircase its distinctive personality.

Treppen

Seit den Anfängen der Menschheit haben Treppen eine konkrete Aufgabe: Höhenunterschiede zwischen Ebenen zu überwinden. Lange Zeit hatten Treppen allein diesen Zweck und waren somit in ihrer Form nur den unmittelbaren Gegebenheiten ihrer Positionierung verpflichtet. Im Laufe der Entwicklung der verschiedenen kulturellen Zivilisationen bildeten sich neue Funktionen aus, die mit der Entstehung bestimmter Gebäudetypen verbunden waren und die Form der Treppe beeinflussten.

Zuerst traten diese neuen Funktionen im sakralen Bereich auf. Hier wurden mit der Treppe mythologische und religiöse Vorstellungen verbunden, die unter anderem Ausdruck des geistigen Strebens nach oben waren. Die Pyramiden der alten Ägypter oder die Bauten der Mayas und Inkas geben noch heute Zeugnis davon. Später kamen repräsentative Aufgaben in profanen Bauten als Ausdruck politischer und wirtschaftlicher Macht hinzu. Dabei gewann die Treppe als Kompositionselement im Gesamtentwurf der Gebäude zunehmend an Bedeutung.

Die Form der Treppe ist jedoch nicht abhängig von den Stilen einzelner Epochen, deren Einfluss sich eher auf den Dekor beschränkt, sondern häufig Ausdruck einer Wertvorstellung oder des Strebens nach technischer Perfektion. Diese Vorstellungen wurden zu einem bedeutenden Motor für die ästhetische und architektonische Entwicklung der Treppe und führte zur Schöpfung herausragender Kunstwerke in allen Kulturen, ohne dass dabei ihre Hauptaufgabe, die Überwindung von Niveauunterschieden, vernachlässigt wurde. Untrennbar mit der Funktion war auch die Wahl des Materials als Bedeutungsträger verbunden, denn seine Kostbarkeit oder die Raffinesse der Konstruktion symbolisierte zugleich den materiellen, gesellschaftlichen und intellektuellen Status des Bauherrn.

14

Mit den Materialien haben sich im Laufe der Zeit auch die Formen der Treppen geändert. Auf Anlagen aus Holz, Lehm und Stroh folgten Steintreppen bis hin zu Konstruktionen aus Stahl und Stahlbeton. Die Bautechnik spielte dabei eine immer wichtigere Rolle, denn sie erlaubte immer kühnere Werke. Einen immensen Fortschritt brachte hier das 19. Jahrhundert mit seinen weitreichenden technischen Verbesserungen. Stahl und Beton erlaubten es weite Räume zu überbauen, und gleichzeitig auf den Aspekt der Sicherheit Rücksicht zu nehmen, z.B. durch die Entwicklung feuerbeständiger Fluchttreppen. Die rationalere Verwendung der Materialien und ihre Kombinationen führten zu einer neuen Formenvielfalt. Die Treppen verloren ihre Steifheit und gewannen an Leichtigkeit durch spiralförmige Silhouetten, dekorative und geschwungene Formen sowie durch die Gestaltung mit verschiedenen Texturen, Beleuchtungselementen und der Aufgliederung des Raumes. Die Treppe wurde gleichsam entmaterialisiert, um ihren Charakter, ihre Linie und die ihr innewohnende Funktion zu bewahren: die des Hinaufsteigens und Hinuntergehens, selbst wenn die Vorstellungskraft zuweilen unausführbare Treppen geschaffen hat; man denke hier nur an den holländischen Künstler M. C. Escher.

Dieses Buch möchte die heutige Vielfalt an Treppen zeigen und den Leser dazu inspirieren, sein Ideal zu finden oder zu erschaffen. Die Ausgangsbasis der Treppe ist die Form; zu Beginn des Werkes werden daher die elementaren Formen anhand von architektonischen Zeichnungen und Fotos erklärt. Das folgende Kapitel behandelt die verschiedenen Materialien: Stein, Holz, Stahlbeton, Metall, Glas und die Kombinationen dieser Materialien. Zum Schluss werden einige Details gezeigt, wie z.B. Geländer und Stufen, um bestimmte Elemente hervorzuheben, die eine Treppe charakterisieren und ihr Persönlichkeit verleihen.

Escaliers

L'escalier est né au commencement de l'humanité avec le propos très concret de surmonter les dénivelés entre les plans. Ce fut longtemps son seul objet et, de ce fait, sa forme était soumise uniquement aux indications directes relatives à son positionnement. Au fil du développement des différentes civilisations culturelles, de nouvelles fonctions se sont révélées, conditionnées par des types d'édifices précis, influant sur la forme de l'escalier.

Ces fonctions surgirent à premier titre dans le cadre du religieux. Les concepts mythologiques et religieux s'y mêlèrent avec l'escalier qui, notamment, concrétisait l'expression de l'élévation spirituelle. Les pyramides de l'ancienne Égypte ou les constructions des Mayas et des Incas en apportent un autre témoignage. Plus tard, des tâches représentatives purent s'y ajouter, dans les constructions profanes, comme une expression du pouvoir politique et économique. L'escalier acquit ainsi, en tant qu'élément de composition, une importance toujours plus conséquente dans les projets de construction.

Mais la forme des escaliers ne dépend pas des styles des diverses époques, dont l'influence se limite en fait à la décoration. Elle symbolise plutôt l'expression d'un ensemble de valeurs ou d'une aspiration à la perfection technique. Ces concepts se sont convertis en une force motrice importante pour le développement esthétique et architectural de l'escalier, à l'origine de la création d'œuvres d'arts extraordinaires au sein de toutes les cultures sans perdre de vue la mission principale : franchir les niveaux. Tout comme la fonction, le choix du matériau se révélait d'importance. En effet sa valeur ou le raffinement de la construction symbolisaient tant la situation matérielle comme la position sociale ou intellectuelle du promoteur.

© Dirk Kurz

Les formes des escaliers ont accompagné les évolutions des matériaux. Des escaliers de paille et d'argile, en passant par ceux en pierre, jusqu'aux constructions en acier et en béton armé. La technique de construction devenant toujours plus essentielle et offrant des possibilités d'édification rivalisant encore d'audace. Le XIXème siècle est une ère de progrès immenses de par ses innovations techniques décisives. Acier et béton armé permettent de couvrir de vastes espaces en respectant en même temps l'aspect sécurité. Ainsi le développement d'escaliers de secours résistants au feu. L'emploi plus rationnel des matériaux de construction et leur combinaison engendrent diverses formes nouvelles. Les escaliers ont perdu leur rigidité et gagné en légèreté à mesure que surgissent les silhouettes en spirale, les formes décoratives et courbes, bien qu'entrent également en jeu les textures, l'éclairage et l'articulation de l'espace. L'on peut avancer que l'escalier s'est peu à peu dématérialisé tout en préservant sa personnalité, ses lignes et sa fonction innée : celle de monter et descendre, bien que l'imagination ait pu engendrer des escaliers impossibles, comme ceux de l'artiste hollandais M.C. Escher.

Ce livre veut dévoiler la diversité actuelle des escaliers et inspirer le lecteur pour qu'il trouve ou crée son escalier idéal. La forme constitue la base fondamentale des escaliers; de ce fait, le texte commence par expliquer les formes les plus élémentaires, illustrées par des dessins architecturaux et des photos. Le chapitre suivant est dédié à la présentation des différents matériaux : pierre, bois, béton armé, métal, verre et leurs combinaisons. À terme, sont proposés quelques détails comme les rampes et marches, afin de mettre en relief certains éléments distinctifs d'un escalier lui conférant sa personnalité.

Escaleras

Las escaleras existen desde los albores de la humanidad con un fin muy concreto, salvar desniveles entre planos. Y así fue durante un largo periodo de tiempo, en el que únicamente cumplieron este cometido funcional. Por ello, su forma sólo dependía del espacio en el que se ubicaran. Sin embargo, con el transcurso de las diferentes civilizaciones, fueron perfilándose nuevos condicionantes y funciones.

En un primer momento, estas funciones surgieron en el ámbito de la religión, donde la escalera se asoció con los conceptos mitológicos y religiosos. Entre otros significados, las escaleras materializaban la expresión del ascenso espiritual. Las pirámides de los antiguos egipcios o las edificaciones de los mayas testimonian, aún hoy, este contenido. Posteriormente, adquirieron una funcionalidad representativa en edificios profanos, como expresión del poder político y económico. Con ello, iban ganando cada vez mayor importancia como elemento compositivo en la proyección de las edificaciones.

La forma de la escalera, sin embargo, no depende de los estilos artísticos de las diferentes épocas, cuya influencia se limita a los aspectos decorativos, sino que simboliza frecuentemente la expresión de unos valores o la aspiración de la perfección técnica. Estos conceptos se convirtieron en una importante fuerza motriz para el desarrollo estético y arquitectónico de la escalera, y son el origen de la creación de extraordinarias obras de arte en todas las culturas, aunque sin olvidar nunca su función principal, superar desniveles. Un aspecto inseparable de la funcionalidad es la elección del material de construcción, ya que tanto su valor como el refinamiento constructivo simbolizaban la posición económica, social e intelectual del promotor.

Los materiales han ido evolucionando y, con ellos, las formas de las escaleras. Desde el uso de arcilla y paja, pasando por la piedra, se llega a la construcción de acero y al empleo de hormigón armado. La técnica constructiva ha ido desempeñando un papel de creciente importancia, y ha permitido edificaciones cada vez más audaces. En esta cuestión, el siglo XIX supuso un gran progreso con sus extensas mejoras técnicas. Acero y hormigón permitían cubrir amplios espacios, respetando al mismo tiempo la seguridad, como es el caso de las escaleras de emergencia resistentes al fuego. La utilización más racional de los materiales de construcción y su combinación conllevó una nueva variedad de formas. Las escaleras perdieron su rigidez y ganaron ligereza al surgir las siluetas en espiral y las formas decorativas y curvas, al tiempo que fueron entrando en juego las diferentes texturas, la iluminación y la articulación del espacio. Así, la escalera se ha ido desmaterializando para conservar su carácter, sus líneas y su función innata: la de subir y bajar, aunque la imaginación haya llegado a concebir escaleras imposibles, como las del artista holandés M. C. Escher.

Este libro quiere mostrar la diversidad actual de escaleras e inspirar al lector para que encuentre o cree su escalera ideal. La forma es la base que fundamenta las escaleras; por ello, al comienzo de la obra se explican las formas más elementales, ilustradas con dibujos arquitectónicos y fotos. El siguiente capítulo está dedicado a la presentación de los diferentes materiales: piedra, madera, hormigón armado, metal, vidrio y combinaciones de estos materiales. Finalmente, se muestran algunos detalles, como las barandillas y los escalones, para destacar ciertos elementos que distinguen a una escalera y le confieren personalidad.

Types
Formen
Formes
Formas

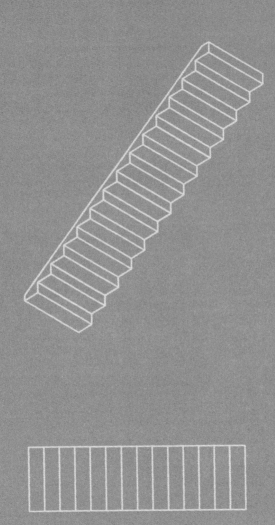

Single-flight staircases

Einläufige Treppen

Escaliers d'une seule volée

Escaleras de un tramo

Single-flight staircases are ones with steps that succeed each other without any interruption. They are usually straight but they can also incorporate a change of direction (in which case the steps will compensate for the deviation). This type of staircase is normally used when the gap between the levels is short, allowing users to go up or down without any need to stop for a rest.

Single-flight cases are the most common kind of staircase in houses, as they are easy to build and the height between the levels does not demand any long climbs. There is no limitation as regards materials, and so the final choice depends entirely on the tastes and budget of the architect and client, although wood and steel are the most frequently used, on account of their lightness.

The minimum possible width is 20 inches, but if space permits it is advisable to install a staircase at least 32 inches in width.

Einläufige Treppen

Single-flight staircases

Bei einläufigen Treppen sind die Stufen in einer fortlaufenden Reihe angeordnet. Normalerweise verlaufen sie in gerader Richtung, eine Richtungsänderung ist jedoch nicht ausgeschlossen; in diesem Fall wird die Drehung der Stufen kompensiert. Dieser Treppentyp wird für gewöhnlich bei niedrigen Niveauunterschieden verwendet, so dass die Benutzer beim Hinauf- oder Hinuntergehen nicht zum Ausruhen stehenbleiben müssen.

Einläufige Treppen werden wegen ihrer problemlosen Bauweise vorzugsweise in Wohnungen eingebaut, da hier die Höhe der Niveaudifferenzen keinen langen Aufstieg erfordert. Es gibt keine Materialbeschränkungen; die Auswahl hängt ausschließlich vom Geschmack und Kostenvoranschlag des Architekten und des Kunden ab, obwohl Holz und Stahl wegen der von ihnen vermittelten Leichtigkeit am häufigsten verwendet werden.

Die Breite kann bis auf 50 cm reduziert werden, es empfiehlt sich aber, Treppen mit einer Mindestbreite von 80 cm zu installieren, wenn ausreichend Platz zur Verfügung steht.

Les escaliers d'une seule volée voient les marches se succéder sans aucune interruption. Ils sont normalement droits, mais peuvent également incorporer des changements de sens ; en ce cas, les marches de l'angle seront compensées. Ce type d'escalier se rencontre le plus souvent lorsque le dénivelé est faible, les usagers pouvant monter et descendre sans nécessiter un arrêt pour se reposer.

Les escaliers d'une seule volée sont les plus courants dans les logements, de par leur facilité de construction mais aussi en raison de dénivelés n'impliquant pas de longues ascensions. Il n'existe aucune restriction en regard des matériaux employés et le choix est uniquement soumis aux goûts et au budget de l'architecte et du client. Cependant le bois et l'acier, en raison de leur légèreté, sont les plus employés.

Leur largeur peut se réduire à 50 cm mais, avec un peu plus d'espace, seuls devraient être installés des escaliers de 80 cm pour le moins.

Escaliers d'une seule volée

Escaleras de un tramo

Las escaleras de un tramo son aquellas en las que los peldaños se suceden sin ninguna interrupción. Suelen ser rectas, aunque también pueden incorporar algún cambio de sentido; en este caso, se compensarán los peldaños del giro. Este tipo de escaleras se acostumbra a utilizar cuando el desnivel es reducido, por lo que los usuarios pueden ascender o descender sin necesidad de pararse a descansar.

Las escaleras de un tramo son las más usuales en viviendas, por su fácil construcción y porque la altura de los desniveles no exige largas ascensiones. No hay restricción en cuanto a materiales, y la elección está sujeta sólo a los gustos y presupuesto de arquitecto y cliente, aunque la madera y el acero, por la ligereza que confieren, son los más empleados.

La anchura puede reducirse hasta los 50 cm, pero si se dispone de espacio, se debería instalar escaleras de unos 80 cm como mínimo.

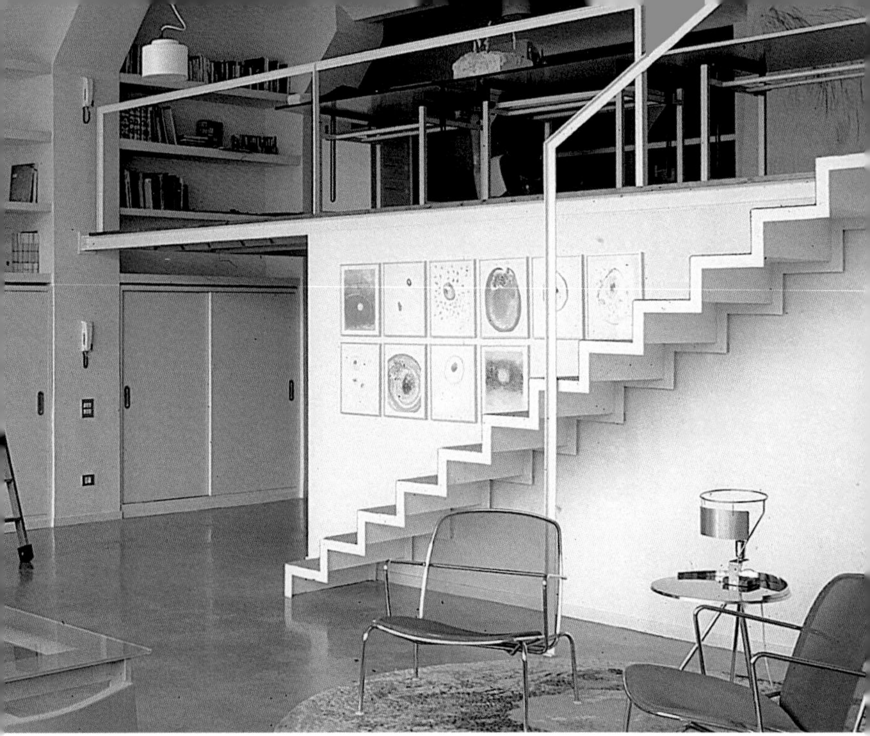

© Pere Planells (2 photos)

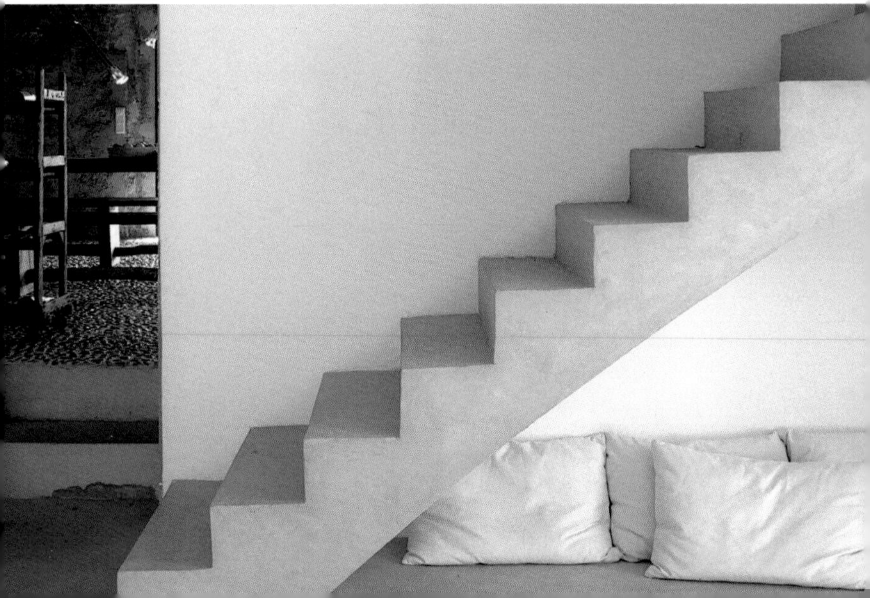

© Eugeni Pons

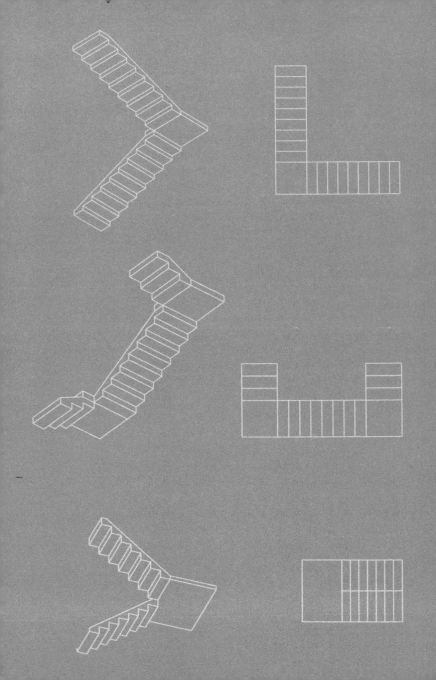

Multi-flight staircases

Mehrläufige Treppen/ Podesttreppen

Escaliers de plusieurs volées

Escaleras de varios tramos

Multi-flight staircases combine series of steps with rest areas and changes in direction. They predominate in public buildings, as they facilitate the passage between great heights and can be adapted according to the different spaces through which they pass. Moreover, their configuration sometimes makes it possible to put an elevator shaft in the middle of the flights, thereby centralizing the vertical communication within a confined area.

In some cases, compensated staircases are built to reduce the amount of space taken up, with trapezoidal steps wherever there is a change of direction, to take the fullest advantage of the surface area available.

The flights of these staircases should be at least 32 inches (80 cm) wide in family homes. When public facilities are involved, it is essential to consult the building regulations prevailing in a particular country for the type of staircase required; these are based on the resistance of materials to fire and the number of floors and users in the building.

Multi-flight staircases

Mehrläufige Treppen/Podesttreppen

Bei mehrläufigen Treppen/Podesttreppen werden mehrere Treppenläufe mit Zwischenpodesten und Richtungsänderungen kombiniert. Ihre Verwendung eignet sich besonders für öffentliche Gebäude, da sie die Verbindung zwischen großen Höhenunterschieden ermöglichen und sich an die unterschiedlichen Installationsgegebenheiten anpassen. Zuweilen besteht je nach Anordnung die Möglichkeit, im Zentrum der Läufe einen Aufzug zu installieren und so alle vertikalen Verbindungen auf eine reduzierte Fläche zu konzentrieren.

Mit dem Ziel der Platzreduzierung werden gelegentlich halb- oder viertelgewendelte Treppen mit trapezförmigen Stufen an den Richtungswechseln gebaut, um die Drehungsfläche optimal zu nutzen.

Die Mindestbreite dieser Treppen in Einfamilienhäusern sollte 80 cm betragen. Bei öffentlichen Gebäuden müssen die Konstruktionsvorschriften jedes Landes für die verschiedenen Typen berücksichtigt werden, die auf der Feuerbeständigkeit der Materialien, der Anzahl der Etagen und Benutzer des Gebäudes basieren.

Les escaliers comportant plusieurs volées combinent des suites de marches avec des paliers et des changements de sens. On les retrouve surtout dans les bâtiments publics, puisqu'ils facilitent le franchissement d'importantes élévations et s'adaptent aux différents lieux où ils sont situés. Par surcroît, leur disposition permet dans certains cas d'installer un ascenseur entre les volées de marche et, par ce biais, de centraliser toutes les communications verticales sur une superficie réduite.

Parfois, pour réduire l'espace occupé, sont édifiés des escaliers compensés dont les marches adoptent une forme trapézoïdale lors des changements de sens, afin de profiter au mieux de la superficie de l'angle.

La largeur des volées de ces escaliers ne devrait pas être inférieure à 80 cm pour les maisons particulières. Pour les édifices publics, il s'avère nécessaire de consulter les normes de construction de chaque pays pour les différentes typologies, en fonction de la résistance au feu des matériaux ainsi que du nombre d'étages et d'usagers du bâtiment.

Escaleras de varios tramos

Escaliers de plusieurs volées

Las escaleras de varios tramos combinan peldaños seguidos con descansillos y giros de sentido. Son las más utilizadas en edificios públicos, ya que facilitan el recorrido entre grandes alturas y se adaptan a las distintas estancias donde se colocan. Además, en algunos casos su disposición permite instalar un ascensor en medio de los tramos y, de este modo, centralizar todas las comunicaciones verticales en una superficie reducida.

En ocasiones, para reducir el espacio ocupado, se construyen escaleras compensadas donde los peldaños tienen forma trapezoidal en los cambios de sentido para aprovechar al máximo la superficie del giro.

La anchura de los tramos de estas escaleras debería ser de 80 cm como mínimo en viviendas unifamiliares. En cuanto a los edificios públicos, se debe consultar la normativa constructiva de cada país para las distintas tipologías, que se basa en la resistencia al fuego de los materiales y el número de plantas y de usuarios del edificio.

Spiral staircases

Wendel- und Spindeltreppen

Escaliers en colimaçon

Escaleras de caracol

Spiral staircases are the best option when communication is required between two levels within a confined space. A circular ascent forgoes long, straight sloping flights for a more vertical thrust, so although less space is taken up, users have to make a greater effort and there is a loss of safety and comfort. This means that spiral staircases should not be used for heights of more than 13 feet.

Spiral staircases are made up of a series of elements which can be easily assembled: the inner edge of the treads fit into a central axis or pole while the outer part is left free to hold the vertical supports of the banister. The width of circular staircases ranges from 20 to 40 inches, although there are some with a diameter of up to 10 feet in diameter, but in these the pole is substituted by an empty cylindrical space commonly known as the eye of the staircase.

Spiral staircases

Wendel- und Spindeltreppen

Wendeltreppen sind die beste Alternative, wenn zwei Ebenen unter größter Platzeinsparung miteinander verbunden werden sollen. Beim rundläufigen Aufstieg werden die Stufen nicht auf geneigte geradlinige Läufe gestützt, um die Vertikalität zu erreichen; dadurch wird der Raumbedarf zwar verringert, die Belastung der Benutzer jedoch durch den Verlust von Sicherheit und Bequemlichkeit vergrößert. Diese Treppen sollten daher bei Höhenunterschieden von über vier Metern nicht verwendet werden.

Wendel- und Spindeltreppen bestehen aus einer Reihe von Elementen, die leicht zusammengebaut werden können: die Stufen werden an eine zentrale Achse oder Säule (Spindel) montiert, wobei die Innenseiten der Trittflächen übereinander gesetzt werden und die Außenseiten zur Abstützung der Geländerträger dienen.

Die Breite dieser Treppen schwankt zwischen 50 cm und einem Meter. Es werden jedoch auch Treppen mit einem Durchmesser von bis zu drei Meter gebaut, bei denen die Spindel durch einen zylindrischen Freiraum ersetzt wird, der üblicherweise als Treppenauge bezeichnet wird.

Les escaliers en colimaçon constituent la meilleure option pour établir une communication entre deux niveaux, tout en occupant un espace minimal. L'ascension circulaire se libère de l'appui de ses éléments sur des plans droits inclinés pour tendre à la verticalité. Si l'espace occupé est moindre, l'effort des usagers augmente et ceux-ci doivent abandonner sécurité et confort. Pour cette raison, ces escaliers ne devraient pas être envisagés pour des dénivelés supérieurs à quatre mètres.

Les escaliers en colimaçon sont composés d'une série d'éléments d'assemblage facile : les échelons s'accouplent à un axe central superposant la partie intérieure des marches et dégageant la partie excentrée pour appuyer les montants de la rampe.

La largeur de ces escaliers circulaires oscille entre 50 cm et un mètre. L'on peut également construire des escaliers atteignant 3 m de diamètre. À leur axe se substitue un espace cylindrique vide, communément dénommé œil de l'escalier.

Escaleras de caracol

Escaliers en colimaçon

Las escaleras de caracol son la mejor opción cuando se quiere comunicar dos niveles ocupando el mínimo espacio. Con la ascensión circular se deja de apoyar los elementos en tramos rectos inclinados para tender a la verticalidad, por lo que si bien el espacio ocupado es más pequeño, el esfuerzo de los usuarios es mayor, perdiendo éstos seguridad y confort. Por ello, estas escaleras no deberían utilizarse en desniveles que superen los cuatro metros.

Las escaleras de caracol se componen de una serie de elementos que se ensamblan fácilmente: los peldaños se acoplan a un eje central o mástil superponiendo la parte interior de la huella y dejando la exterior para apoyar los montantes de la barandilla.

La anchura de las escaleras circulares oscila entre los 50 cm y un metro. También se construyen escaleras de hasta 3 m de diámetro, pero en éstas se sustituye el mástil por un espacio cilíndrico vacío comúnmente denominado ojo de la escalera.

© Matteo Piazza

© Eugeni Pons

© Pere Planells

© Dirk Kurz

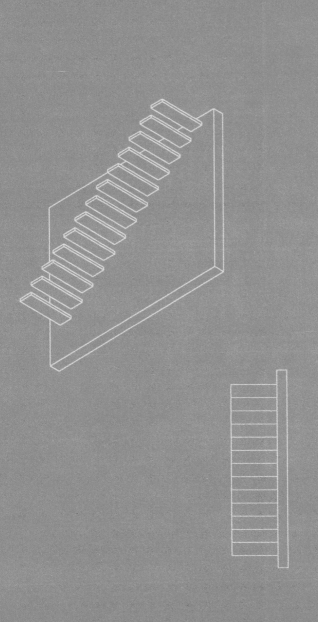

Steps fixed to a wall

Freitragende in der Wand eingebundene Treppen

Escaliers fixés au mur

Escalones fijados al muro

Staircases with steps fixed to the wall occupy little space – only the width of the treads – and so they are mainly used in houses. They lack any overall structural system, as each step is fixed to the wall by means of independent metal clamps. Traditionally the steps used to be embedded into the wall, but nowadays the thinness of partitions and the appearance of new techniques have caused this method to fall into disuse.

Staircases of this type are classified according to the material of the steps. Wood – treated with varnish so that woodworm or other insects do not weaken its resistance – is one of the materials most widely used as it is light and has a homely look. Plywood has the same qualities and is cheaper. Stone or concrete steps are out of the question as they are too heavy.

Steps fixed to a wall

Freitragende in der Wand eingebundene Treppen

Treppen aus ausschließlich in der Wand freitragend befestigten Trittstufen nehmen wenig Platz ein, d. h. nur die Breite der Stufe, und werden daher hauptsächlich für Wohnungen verwendet. Sie verfügen über keine zusammenhängende Struktur, da sie an der Wand mit voneinander unabhängigen Metallverankerungen befestigt werden. Früher wurden sie in die Wand eingelassen, wobei die Hälfte der Stufe im Innenraum der Wandscheibe eingebettet wurde; heute wird diese Technik aufgrund der geringen Stärke der Zwischenwände und infolge des Aufkommens neuer Techniken nur noch selten angewendet.

Die Treppen dieser Art werden nach dem Material der Stufen klassifiziert. Eines der wegen seines geringen Gewichtes und seiner warmen Tönung am häufigsten verwendeten Materialien ist gegen Holzwurm und Insekten geschütztes Holz. Furniere bieten gleiche Vorteile und sind preisgünstiger. Stufen aus Stein oder Beton können nicht verwendet werden, weil sie zu schwer sind.

Les escaliers dont les marches sont fixées au mur occupent un espace faible, réduit à la largeur de l'échelon, et sont donc relativement fréquents dans les logements. Ces escaliers sont dépourvus de système structurel commun, étant ancrés dans le mur par des fixations métalliques indépendantes. Les escaliers étaient auparavant incorporés au mur, les marches étant pour moitié enchâssées dans la paroi, mais la faible épaisseur actuelle des séparations conjuguée à l'apparition de nouvelles techniques ont accéléré l'obsolescence de cette technique. Les escaliers de ce type sont classifiés en fonction des matériaux employés pour les échelons. Le bois, vernis afin d'éviter les détériorations engendrées par les insectes et notamment les vermoulures, est un des matériaux les plus prisés en raison de sa légèreté et de son apparence chaude. Le contreplaqué offre les mêmes prestations mais se révèle plus économique. Les escaliers en pierre et en béton doivent être écartés, étant trop pesants.

Escalones fijados al muro

Escaliers fixés au mur

Las escaleras de peldaños fijados al muro ocupan poco espacio, sólo el ancho de la pieza, por lo que se utilizan mayoritariamente en viviendas. Carecen de un sistema estructural conjunto, ya que se fijan al muro mediante anclajes metálicos independientes. Antiguamente se empotraban en la pared, embebiendo la mitad del peldaño en el interior de la partición, pero hoy en día el escaso grosor de los tabiques y la aparición de nuevas técnicas ha llevado a ésta sea una técnica en desuso.

Las escaleras de este tipo se clasifican según el material de los peldaños. La madera, tratada con barnices para que la carcoma o los insectos no deterioren su resistencia, es uno de los materiales más utilizados por ser ligera y ofrecer un aspecto cálido. El contrachapado tiene las mismas prestaciones y es más económico. Se descartan los peldaños de piedra y hormigón por ser demasiado pesados.

© Juan Rodríguez

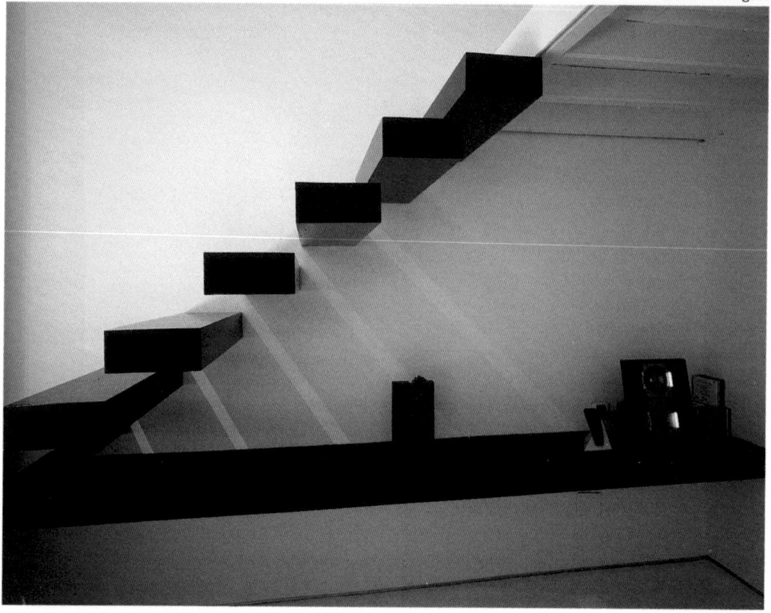

© Patrik Engquist

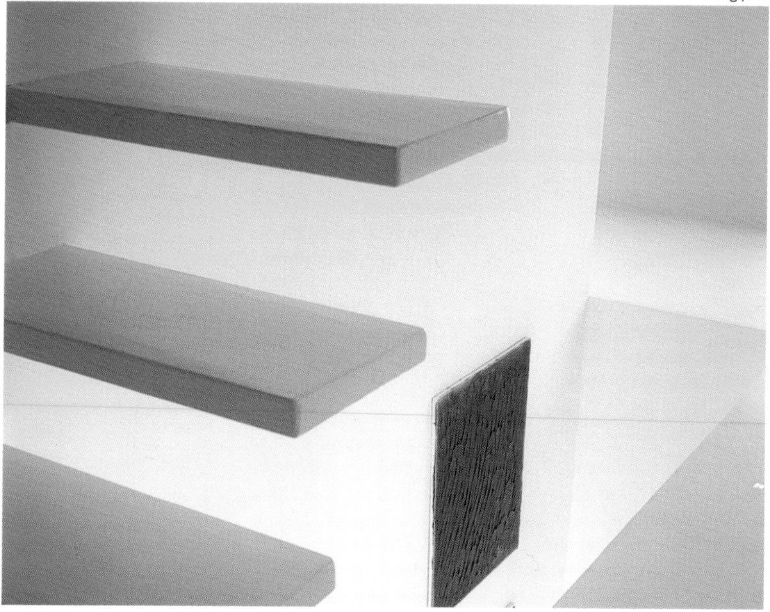

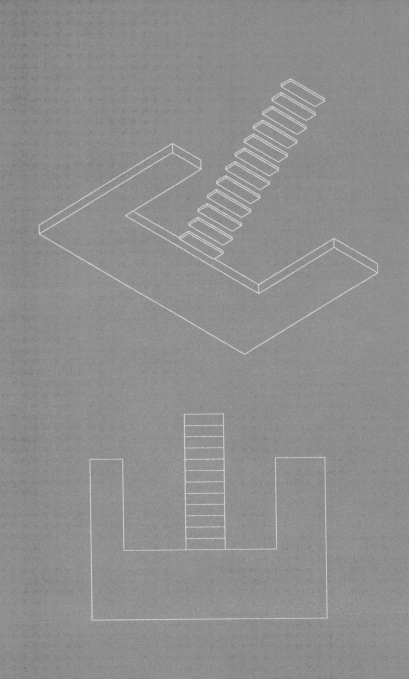

Free-standing staircases

Freitragende Treppen

Escaliers libres

Escaleras exentas

In some buildings the staircase is a sculptural component that is a focal point of the space, separated from the walls and standing on its own, ready not only to be used but also to be admired. They are displayed in public buildings as a design feature but they must be complemented by enclosed staircases because they do not satisfy with building regulations, as they are directly exposed in the event of a fire.

The structural system holding them up is always supported from the upper story and consists of one shaft underneath the central part of the steps or two at the sides. The banister, which sometimes starts in the ceiling, also constitutes a structural element that supports the steps.

The materials chosen for this type of staircase are often very eye-catching. Combinations of wood, cement and metals like stainless steel and aluminum result in highly imaginative staircases that evoke an ascent into the realm of the sublime.

Freitragende Treppen

Free-standing staircases

In manchen Gebäuden präsentiert sich die Treppe wie eine Skulptur, wie ein Gestaltungselement des Raumes; abgesetzt von den Mauern strebt sie frei nach oben, um sowohl den Benutzern zu dienen als auch von ihnen bewundert zu werden. In öffentlichen Gebäuden werden sie als repräsentativer Entwurf installiert, müssen jedoch durch geschlossene Treppen ergänzt werden, da die Freitreppen direkt dem Feuer ausgesetzt sind und daher nicht den Sicherheitsnormen entsprechen.

Das Tragsystem stützt sich immer auf die obere Decke und besteht aus einem Profil unter dem Mittelteil der Stufen oder aus zwei seitlichen Profilen oder Wangen. Das Geländer kann sogar von der Decke abgehängt sein und so ein Strukturelement bilden, das die Stufen trägt. Die Materialauswahl für diese Art von Treppen ist überaus vielfältig. Die Kombination von Holz, Metall, wie z. B. Edelstahl oder Aluminium, und Beton ermöglicht äußerst phantasievolle Treppengestaltungen, die den Eindruck einer Annäherung an das Erhabene entstehen lassen.

64

Certains édifices voient l'escalier se dresser comme un composant sculptural, tel un élément organisant l'espace, en se détachant des murs et en s'élevant pour que les usagers puissent tant l'utiliser que l'admirer. Ils s'intègrent aux bâtiments publics comme un avant-goût du design, mais doivent se voir adjoindre des escaliers clos afin de pouvoir répondre aux contraintes réglementaires, étant eux-mêmes directement exposés au feu.

Le système structurel qui les sous-tend s'appuie toujours sur la voûte supérieure et est composé d'un profil, sous la partie centrale des marches, ou de deux profils latéraux. La main courante, qui parfois s'élance depuis le toit, constitue également un élément structurel supportant les marches.

Le choix des matériaux est, pour ce type d'escalier, habituellement exubérant. La combinaison de bois, de métaux, comme l'acier inoxydable ou l'aluminium, et de béton donne naissance à des escaliers particulièrement imaginatifs qui peuvent évoquer l'ascension vers le sublime.

Escaleras exentas

Escaliers libres

En algunos edificios la escalera se erige como un componente escultórico, como el elemento organizador del espacio, por lo que se despega de los muros y se levanta exenta para que los usuarios la puedan utilizar y también admirar. En los edificios públicos se colocan como reclamo de diseño, pero deben complementarse con escaleras cerradas puesto que las exentas no cumplen ninguna normativa al estar directamente expuestas al fuego.

El sistema estructural que las sustenta se apoya siempre en el forjado superior y está compuesto por un perfil bajo la parte central de los peldaños o por dos en los laterales. La barandilla, que a veces arranca del techo, también se constituye en elemento estructural que soporta los peldaños.

La elección de materiales acostumbra a ser, en este tipo de escaleras, exuberante. La combinación de maderas, de metales como el acero inoxidable o el aluminio, y de hormigón conforma escaleras muy imaginativas que llegan a evocar la ascensión a lo sublime.

Materials
Materialien
Materiaux
Materiales

Metal staircases
Metalltreppen
Escaliers métalliques
Escaleras metálicas

Metal, a material extensively used in construction ever since the Industrial Revolution, has evolved over time and now serves a great many purposes in buildings. Metals or their alloys are suitable for all types and styles of staircase as they are highly malleable elements, although they are generally found in designs with a great purity of line. They look quite light but metal is in fact an extremely solid material. However, the durability of metal structures is dependent on the preliminary treatment applied to prevent rusting, which is especially corrosive outdoors.

Metal staircases are usually made in sections in a workshop and assembled in situ. They can also be prefabricated in one single piece, but their weight must be taken into account when planning transportation and choosing the space to be allocated for their installation. Metal staircases are found in all kinds of architectural contexts but they are particularly used for emergency exits. In a domestic setting, however, the disadvantage of the sound made by footsteps on metal treads cannot be ignored, although this noise can be muffled by the addition of cladding. The metal that is most commonly used is steel, in all its varieties: forged, galvanized or stainless. Aluminum and copper are also found, particularly in the cladding and details in the finishing. Metals can be used in different combinations or complemented by other materials, such as wood. Metal is the ideal material for a robust basic structure supporting steps made with other materials, like wood, for example.

Metall, ein seit der industriellen Revolution häufig beim Bauen verwendetes Material, wurde im Laufe der Zeit weiterentwickelt und wird heute zu den verschiedensten Zwecken gebraucht. Mit Metallen und deren Legierungen können Treppen aller Arten und Stile geschaffen werden, da sie leicht formbar sind. Das Design zeigt im Allgemeinen klare Linien.

Metalltreppen vermitteln trotz der Robustheit des Materials einen schwerelosen Eindruck. Ihre Haltbarkeit hängt jedoch von der Behandlung gegen Rost ab, insbesondere bei Außentreppen. Die Teile der Metalltreppen werden normalerweise in Werkstätten hergestellt und auf der Baustelle zusammengebaut. Sie können auch komplett vorgefertigt werden; für den Transport muss jedoch das Gewicht der einzelnen Elemente berücksichtigt werden sowie der für die Montage verfügbare Platz. Metalltreppen passen sich allen architektonischen Gegebenheiten an und werden vorzugsweise bei Notausgängen eingesetzt. In Wohnungen kann Trittschall störend sein, der durch die Anbringung von Verkleidungen gedämpft werden kann.

Das am häufigsten verwendete Material ist Stahl in allen seinen Erscheinungsformen: geschmiedet, galvanisiert oder als Edelstahl. Aluminium und Kupfer werden in erster Linie für Verkleidungen und Details verwendet. Metalle können miteinander aber auch mit anderen Materialien, wie z. B. mit Holz, kombiniert werden. Sie sind besonders geeignet für solide Grundstrukturen, die dann mit Stufen aus anderen Materialien, z. B. mit Holz verkleidet werden.

Le métal, employé à profusion dans la construction depuis la révolution industrielle, a évolué avec le temps pour être destiné aux usages les plus variés. Les métaux et leurs alliages permettent de construire des escaliers de types et styles divers, en raison de leur grande malléabilité. Le design affiche généralement des lignes pures.

Les escaliers métalliques présentent un aspect léger bien que le métal offre une grande robustesse. Pour autant, le caractère durable des structures métalliques repose sur les traitements préalables contre l'oxydation, plus sévère en extérieurs. Les escaliers métalliques se fabriquent normalement en atelier pour être montés sur l'œuvre. Ils peuvent aussi être entièrement préfabriqués ; mais il faut tenir compte du poids de l'élément lors du transport et du montage dans l'espace prévu.

Bien qu'employés dans tous les types architecturaux, les escaliers métalliques sont privilégiés pour les issues de secours. Pour les particuliers, cependant, il faut garder à l'esprit l'inconvénient de leur sonorité, bien qu'elle puisse être atténuée à l'aide de revêtements.

L'acier est le métal le plus employé, sous toutes ses formes : forgé, galvanisé ou inoxydable. L'aluminium et le cuivre sont essentiellement destinés aux revêtements et aux détails. Les métaux peuvent aisément être associés entre eux ou avec d'autres matériaux, tel le bois. C'est le matériau idéal pour établir une structure de base solide sur laquelle viendront se poser des marches en bois, par exemple.

El metal, material utilizado en construcción profusamente desde la revolución industrial, ha ido evolucionando con el tiempo. Con los metales o sus aleaciones se pueden construir escaleras de todo tipo y estilo, ya que son elementos fácilmente maleables. En general, el diseño es de líneas puras.

Las escaleras metálicas tienen un aspecto ligero, aunque el material ofrece una gran solidez. Sin embargo, su durabilidad de depende de tratamientos previos para evitar la oxidación, que se agudiza si se ubican en el exterior. Se suelen fabricar, por piezas, en talleres y se montan en obra. También pueden ser enteramente prefabricadas; pero hay que tener en cuenta el peso del elemento para su transporte y el espacio previsto que hay para el montaje. Las escaleras metálicas se utilizan en todas las tipologías arquitectónicas, siendo especialmente empleadas para las evacuaciones de emergencia. En las viviendas, sin embargo, debe tenerse en cuenta el inconveniente que supone el sonido que se produce al utilizarlas, que se puede amortiguar mediante la aplicación de revestimientos.

El metal más empleado es el acero, en todas sus modalidades: forjado, galvanizado o inoxidable. El aluminio y el cobre se utilizan, sobre todo, en los revestimientos y en detalles constructivos. Los metales pueden combinarse, bien entre sí, bien con otros materiales, como la madera. Es el material idóneo para construir una sólida estructura de base sobre la cual se colocan los peldaños de otros materiales, p.ej. de madera.

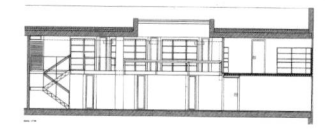

© Lionel Malka (2 photos)

© Peter Cook (2 photos)

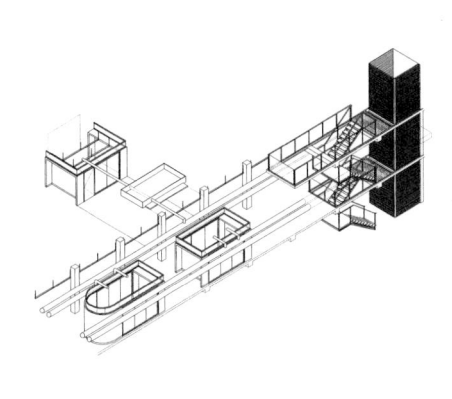

© Oldemar Rivera Casada & Athanasios Haritos (2 photos)

© Sven Everaert (4 photos)

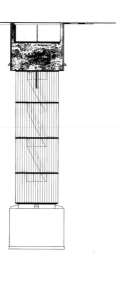

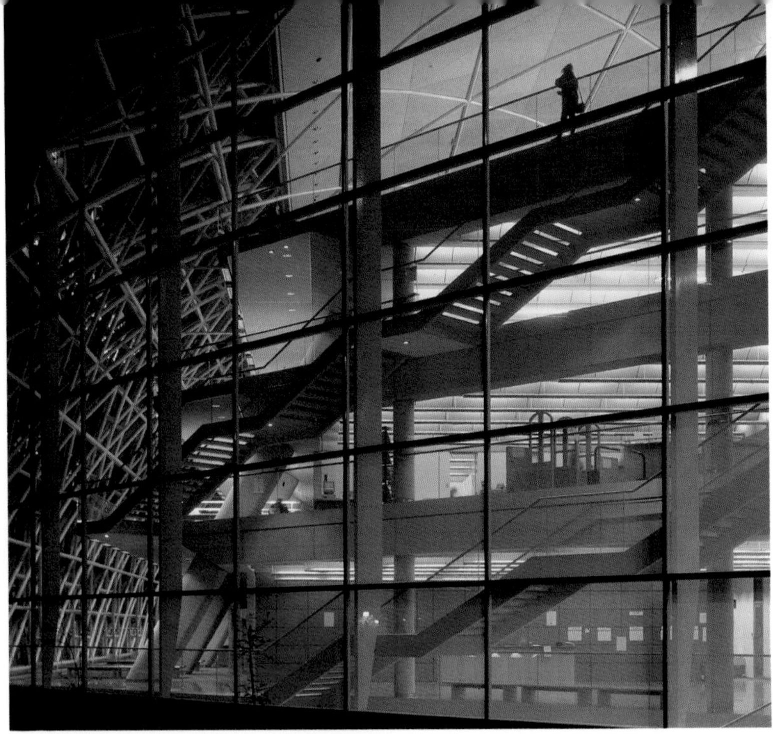

© Herman van Doorn (2 photos)

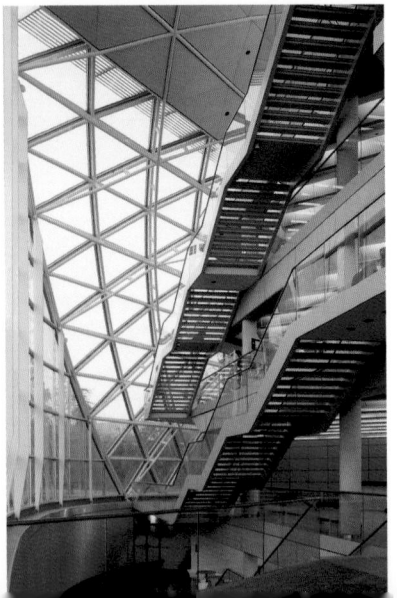

Metal staircases can attain a resistance and subtlety that endow them with sculptural qualities and give them a starring role in a building, over and above their practical function.

Die Kraft und Zartheit der Metalltreppen lassen ihre plastische Gestaltung zu, so dass sie nicht nur nützlich sind, sondern gleichzeitig eine Hauptrolle im Gebäude spielen.

La résistance et la subtilité auxquelles peuvent atteindre les escaliers métalliques leur insufflent des aspects sculpturaux qui, outre leur utilité, leur apportent une importance croissante dans les édifices.

La resistencia y sutilidad que pueden alcanzar las escaleras metálicas permite darles aspectos esculturales que, además de ser útiles, ganan protagonismo en el edificio.

© Duccio Malagamba (4 photos)

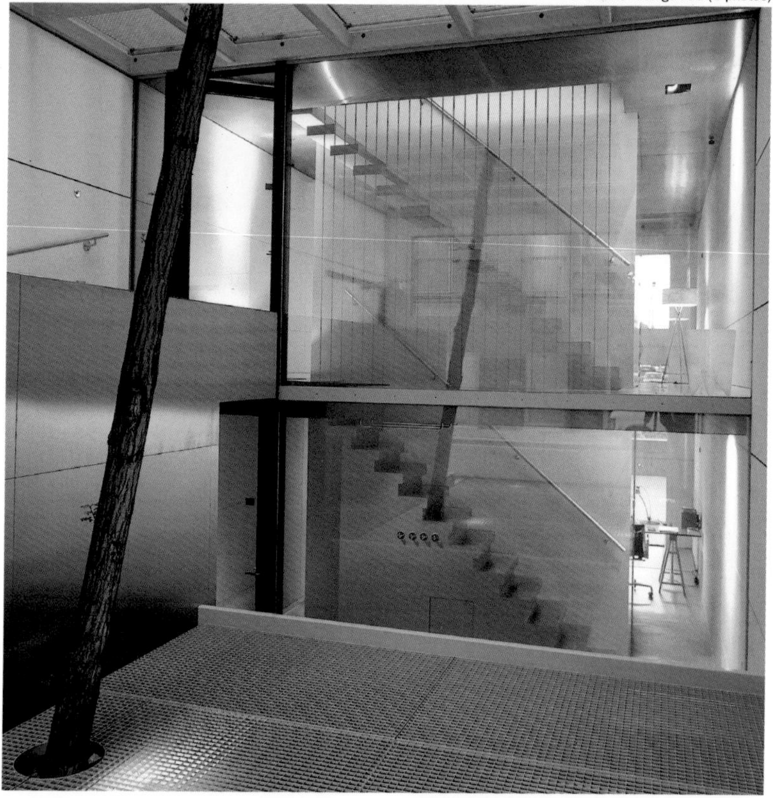

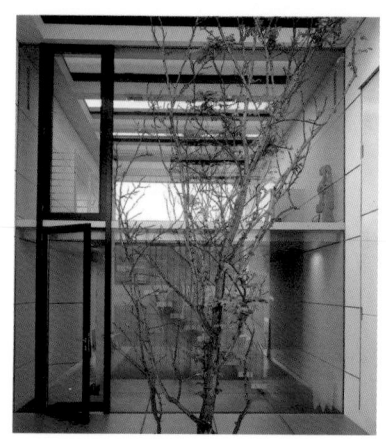

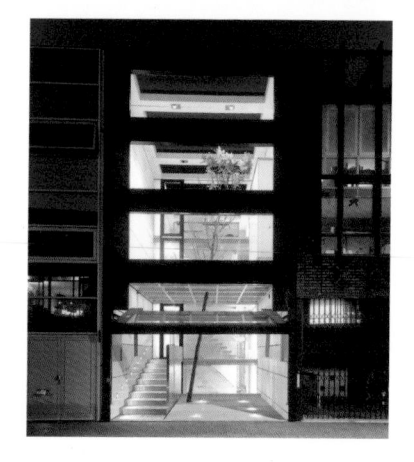

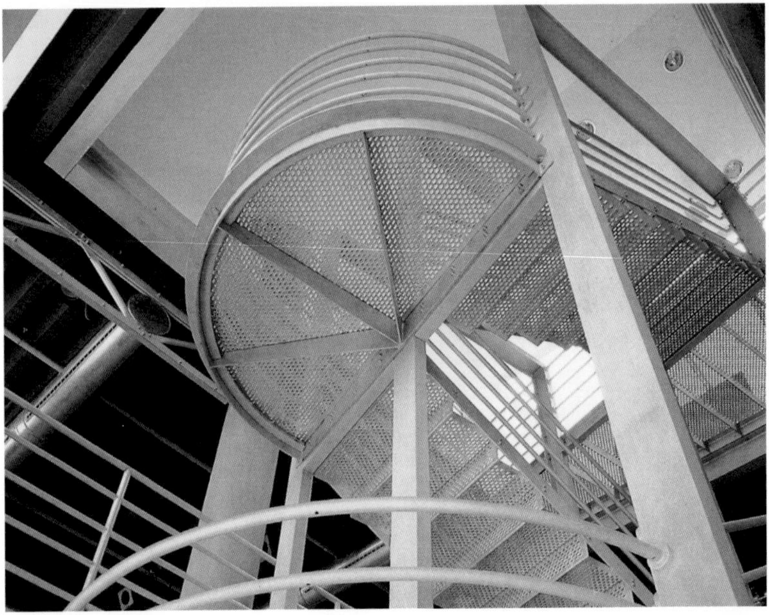

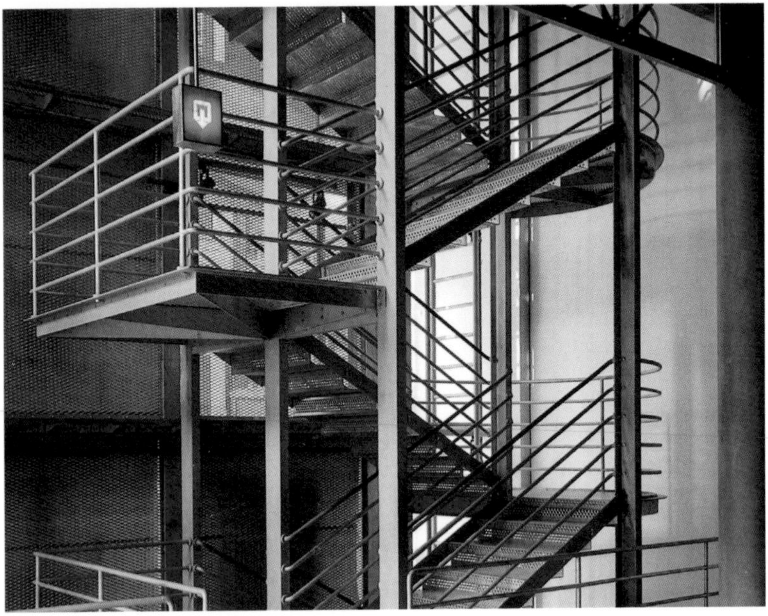

© David Cardelús (4 photos)

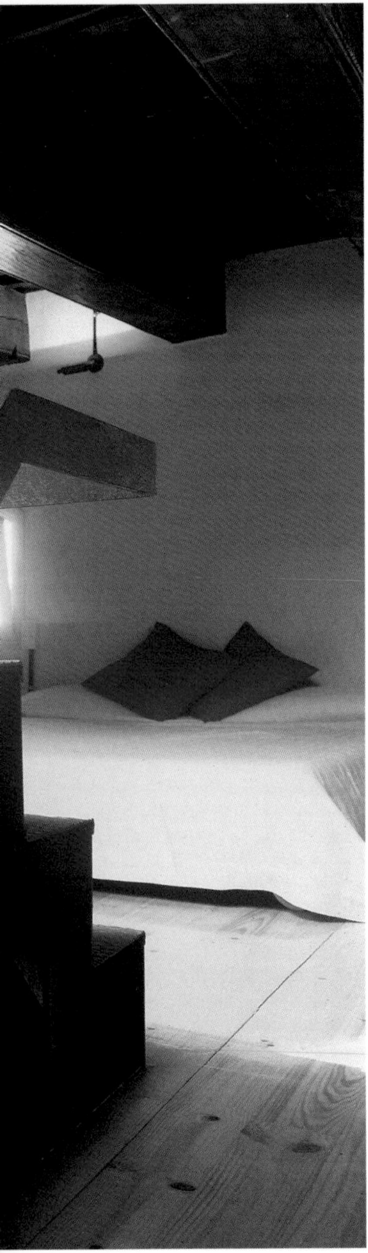

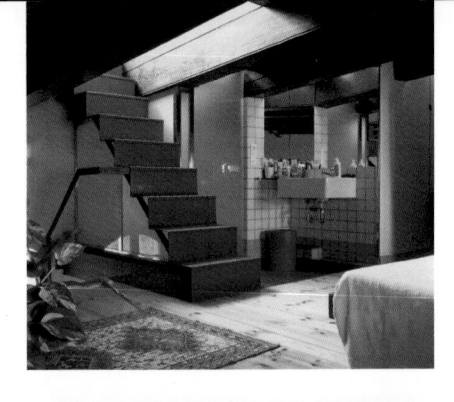

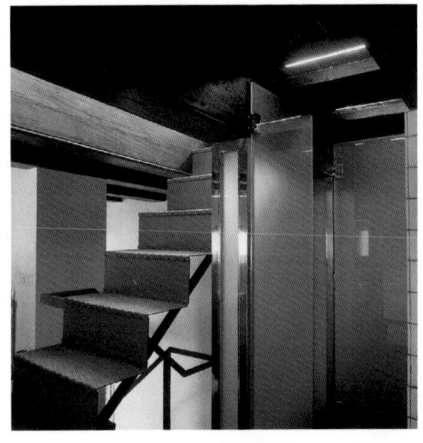

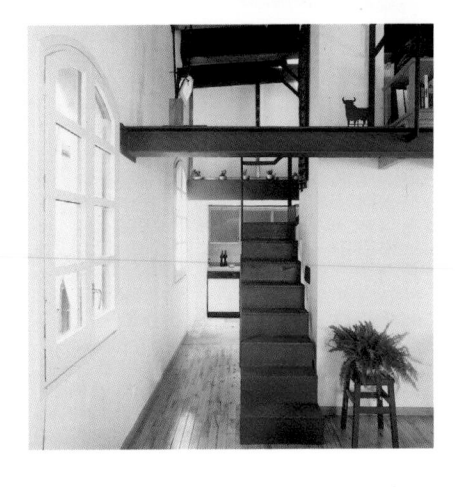

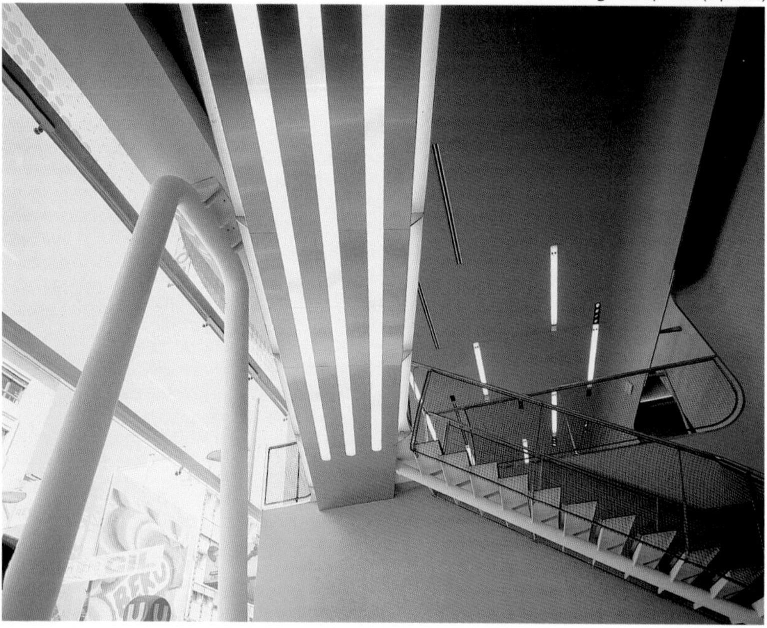

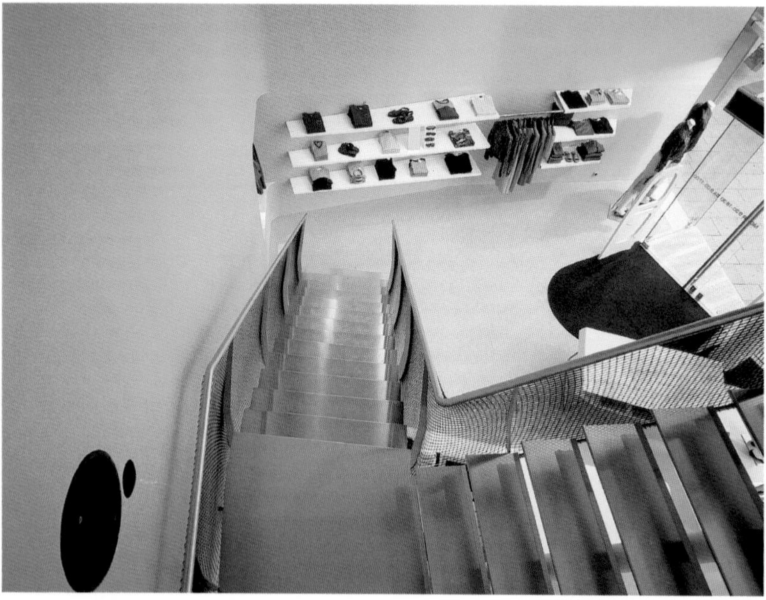

© Jordi Miralles

A well-planned lighting scheme
can emphasize a staircase's
architectural form and the quality
of its materials.

Eine gut durchdachte Beleuchtung
lässt die architektonische Form
und die Materialqualität der Treppe
hervortreten.

Un éclairage bien étudié permet
de souligner la forme
architecturale et la qualité des
matériaux d'un escalier.

Una iluminación bien estudiada
puede destacar la forma
arquitectónica y la calidad de
los materiales de una escalera.

© Andrea Zanzi

The proportions and design of a staircase depend on whether it is intended for public or private use. While the latter can accommodate quite steep gradients, staircases for public use have to meet other requirements, such as a minimum width, maximum gradient and a limited number of steps per flight.

Die Proportionen der Treppe und ihr Verlauf hängen von der Art ihrer Verwendung ab. In Privathäusern können die Neigungen ausgeprägter sein, während in öffentlichen Gebäuden andere Forderungen gestellt werden, wie zum Beispiel die Mindestbreite, die maximale Neigung oder die Stufenanzahl pro Lauf.

Les proportions de l'escalier, ainsi que son développement, dépendent de son objet, public ou privé. Alors que les escaliers privés peuvent atteindre des inclinaisons relativement importantes, ceux destinés au public définissent d'autres exigences comme la largeur minimale, l'inclinaison maximale ou le nombre de marches par volée.

Las proporciones de la escalera, y su desarrollo, dependen de su uso público o privado. Mientras que las de uso privado pueden llegar a inclinaciones bastante fuertes, las de uso público definen otras exigencias como el ancho mínimo, la inclinación máxima o el número de escalones por tramo.

© Reiner Blunck

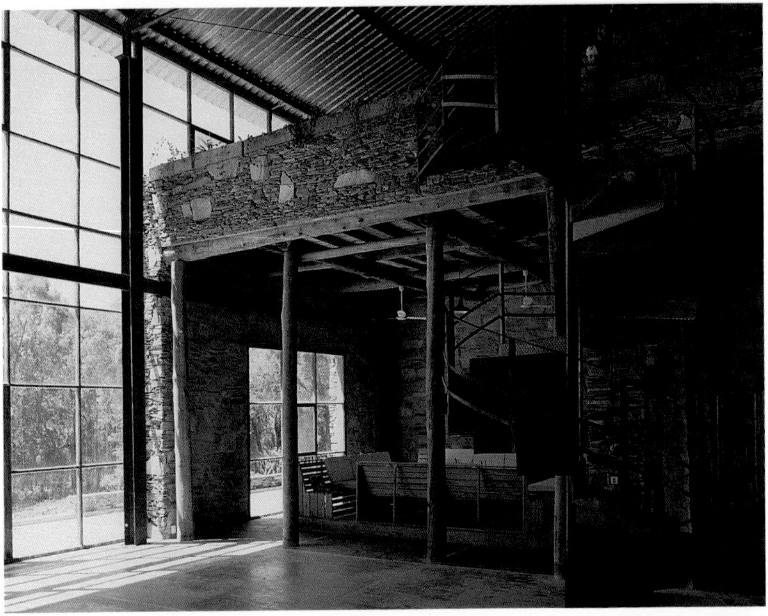

© Undine Pröhl (2 photos)

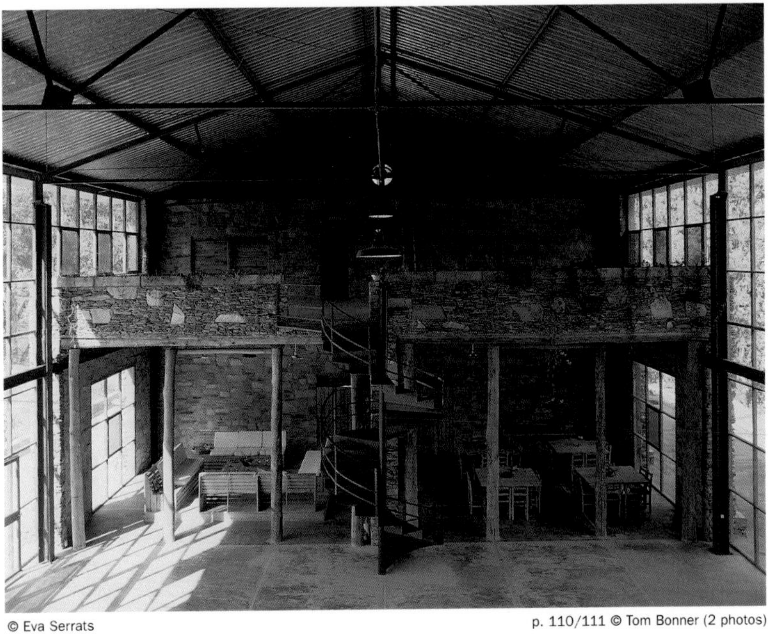

© Eva Serrats

p. 110/111 © Tom Bonner (2 photos)

The curved banister on the upper level provides a striking echo of the visual statement made by the staircase.

Das geschwungene Geländer aus Stahl verstärkt und betont die Ästhetik der Treppe.

Curviligne, la main courante prolonge et accentue l'esthétique de l'escalier.

La barandilla del forjado en forma de curva continúa y enfatiza la estética de la escalera.

Wooden staircases
Holztreppen
Escaliers en bois
Escaleras de madera

Wood – along with mud and straw – was one of the first materials used to build staircases. It is natural, accessible, abundant and cheap. Over the centuries, carpenters and cabinet-makers have diligently refined their craftsmanship and as a result of their endeavors a wide variety of finishes are now available. Wood is a warm material that blends in easily anywhere, and so wooden staircases can be put into all types of setting – whether rustic, modern or even minimalist. The finish that is chosen – varnish, enamel, wax, etc. – is crucial to the end result. Wooden staircases are mainly used in interiors, but it is always advisable to opt for hard woods such as oak, ash and exotic woods. Gluing together several layers of wood is another way of increasing its resistance. Wooden staircases can also be put up outdoors, although they must be given a protective treatment, unless they are made of woods like teak or iroko. Wooden staircases require care and maintenance if they are used intensively.

Wood is sometimes used merely to clad a metal or concrete structure, thereby endowing it with warmth and elegance. The wood on a floor or wall cladding can also be extended onto the steps of a staircase to unify or harmonize a setting.

Different types of wood can be combined, or wood can complement other materials, especially metal. It is necessary to place bands of non-slip material, such as rough stone or rubber, on the front edge of the treads, to eliminate the risk of sliding on the smooth surface of the wood.

Holz ist – zusammen mit Lehm und Stroh – das älteste Material für den Treppenbau. Es ist ein natürliches Material, leicht zu beschaffen, reichlich vorhanden und günstig. Jahrhundertelang haben Schreiner und Kunsttischler wertvolle künstlerische Werke in vielfältigen Ausführungen geschaffen. Treppen aus Holz – ein warmes und harmonisches Material – passen in alle Umgebungen, rustikal, modern oder sogar minimalistisch. Der endgültige Eindruck hängt von der gewählten Endbehandlung ab, sei es mit Beize, Lack oder Wachs… Sie werden vorzugsweise für Innenräume verwendet, wobei empfohlen wird, harte Hölzer, wie z. B. Eiche, Buche oder Exoten einzusetzen. Durch das Verleimen mehrerer Holzschichten erhöht sich die Haltbarkeit. Ihre Verwendung im Freien ist ebenfalls möglich, sofern eine Schutzbehandlung vorgenommen wird. Sie ist bei bestimmten Holzarten wie Teak oder Iroko nicht erforderlich. Bei intensiver Benutzung müssen Holztreppen verstärkt gewartet und gepflegt werden. Gelegentlich wird Holz nur als Verkleidung von Beton- oder Metallstrukturen verwendet, um ihnen Eleganz und Wärme zu verleihen. Um die Treppe in die Umgebung einzubinden, kann der Fußbodenbelag oder die Wandverkeidung auf den Stufen fortgesetzt werden. Die verschiedenen Holzarten können miteinander oder mit anderen Materialien, hauptsächlich Metall, eingesetzt werden. Zur Verhinderung der Rutschgefahr auf der Holzfläche wird empfohlen, rutschfeste Streifen, z. B. aus rauhem Stein oder Gummi, vorn an der Trittfläche anzubringen.

Le bois est – comme les constructions d'argile et de paille – le matériau le plus ancien pour les escaliers. Il est naturel, abordable, abondant et économique. Au cours des siècles, menuisiers et ébénistes ont développé une superbe œuvre artisanale donnant naissance à nombre de finitions différentes.

Les escaliers de bois – un matériau chaud et harmonique – peuvent s'intégrer à tout type d'environnement, rustique ou moderne, voire minimaliste. L'apparence définitive est apportée par la finition choisie : vernis, laqué, ciré… Utilisés principalement en intérieur, il est recommandé pour autant de recourir à des bois résistants, comme le chêne, le hêtre ou les essences exotiques. L'encollage de plusieurs couches confère une certaine résistance au bois. Ils peuvent également être destinés à l'extérieur. En ce cas un traitement protecteur est nécessaire, hormis pour certaines essences comme le Teck ou l'Iroko. En cas d'usage intensif, les escaliers de bois requièrent entretien et soins attentifs.

Parfois, le bois est employé uniquement en tant que revêtement pour des structures de béton ou de métal, leur conférant élégance et chaleur. Pour unifier ou harmoniser une atmosphère, le bois peut également être étendu du sol ou des murs sur les marches. Les diverses essences peuvent être combinées entre elles ou avec d'autres matériaux, le métal principalement. Afin d'éviter les risques de glissades sur sa surface, l'emploi de bandes anti-dérapantes est recommandé, en pierre rugueuse ou en gomme, sur le bord avant des échelons.

La madera es, junto con el barro y la paja, el material más antiguo para la construcción de escaleras. Es un material natural, asequible, abundante y económico. Durante siglos, carpinteros y ebanistas han desarrollado un valioso trabajo artesanal que ha dado lugar a una gran variedad de acabados.

Las escaleras de madera, un material cálido y armónico, pueden ubicarse en todo tipo de ambientes, tanto rústico como modernos, e incluso minimalistas. El aspecto definitivo viene dado por el acabado que se elija, ya sea barniz, esmalte, ceras… Se utilizan sobre todo en interiores, pero siempre se recomienda el uso de maderas resistentes, como roble, haya o maderas exóticas. Al encolar varias capas la madera adquiere más resistencia. También se pueden emplear en el exterior, aunque se les debe aplicar un tratamiento protector, exepto a algunas maderas como la Teca o el Iroko. Las escaleras de madera requieren mantenimiento y cuidados en el uso intensivo.

En ocasiones, la madera sólo se utiliza como un revestimiento de las estructuras de hormigón o de metal, que les aporta elegancia y cálidez. Para unificar o armonizar el ambiente también se puede extender el pavimento del suelo o el revestimiento de la pared por los peldaños. Los distintos tipos de madera pueden emplearse entre sí o con distintos materiales, el metal principalmente. Para evitar el riesgo de resbalar en la superficie de la madera, se recomienda colocar bandas antideslizantes, como piedra rugosa o goma, en la parte delantera de las huellas.

Wood offers a whole host of design possibilities: steps in various shapes, with or without a riser. It is also possible to continue the cladding of the steps on the side walls, or use the same wood to build a practical and harmonious banister.

Holz bietet unzählige Designmöglichkeiten: Stufen mit oder ohne Setzstufe und in verschiedenen Formen; ihre Verkleidung kann auch an den Seitenwänden hochgezogen oder es kann aus gleichem Holz ein praktisches und harmonisches Geländer angebracht werden.

Le bois offre une infinité de possibilités conceptuelles : escaliers avec, ou sans, contremarche et de formes diverses ; il permet également de développer le revêtement des marches sur les murs latéraux ou d'utiliser la même essence pour former une main courante, à la fois pratique et en harmonie.

La madera ofrece una infinidad de posibilidades de diseño: escalones con o sin contrahuella y de varias formas; también permite subir el revestimiento de los peldaños por las paredes laterales o utilizar la misma madera para construir una barandilla práctica y armónica.

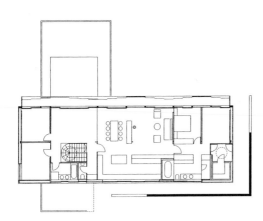

Thin bands of non-slip materials like metal or rubber can be incorporated into the front edges of wooden steps, to avoid the danger of sliding.

Um die Rutschgefahr zu vermeiden, können feine, rutschfeste Streifen aus anderen Materialien, z. B. aus Metall oder Gummi, in die Vorderkanten der Holzstufen integriert werden.

Afin éviter les risques de chute, de fines lignes de matériaux anti-dérapants, comme le métal ou le caoutchouc, peuvent être incorporées sur les bords avants des marches de bois.

Para evitar el peligro de resbalar, se pueden incorporar finas líneas de otros materiales antideslizantes, como el metal o la goma, en los bordes delanteros de los peldaños de madera.

This wooden staircase with several flights creates volumes that play with space, the counterpoint of chiaroscuro and the inverted silhouette of the staircase.

Diese mehrläufige Holztreppe bildet Elemente, die mit dem Raum, den Gegensätzen von hell und dunkel und der Silhouette der invertierten Treppe spielen.

Cet escalier de bois, comportant plusieurs volées, crée des volumes qui jouent avec l'espace, les effets de clair-obscur et sa propre silhouette inversée.

Esta escalera de madera de varios tramos crea volúmenes que juegan con el espacio, la contraposición de claroscuros y la silueta de la escalera invertida.

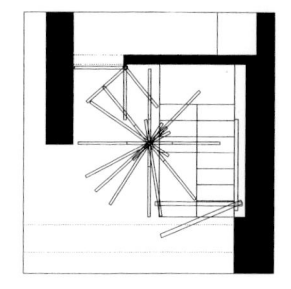

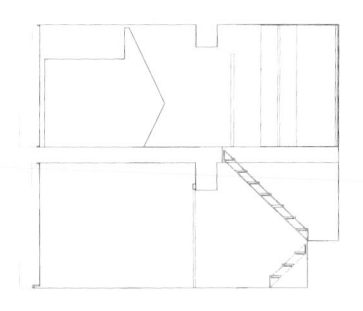

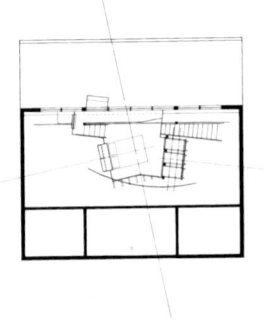
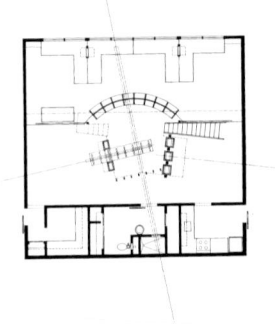

© Peter Kerze

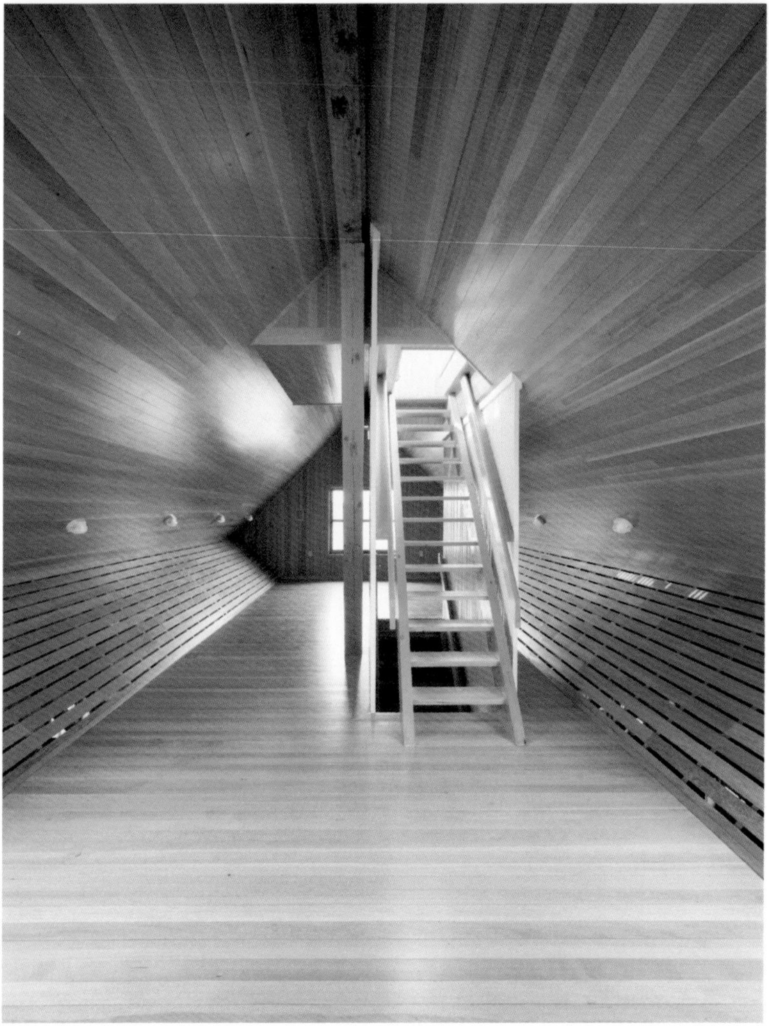

p. 140-141 © Peter Kerze (3 photos)

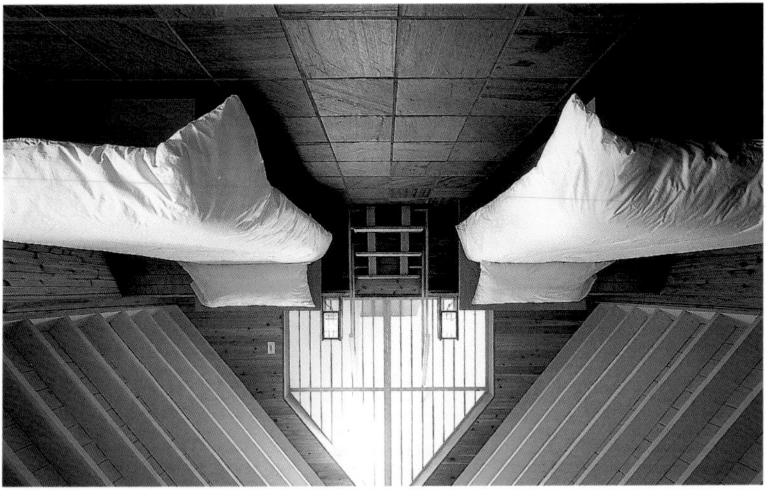

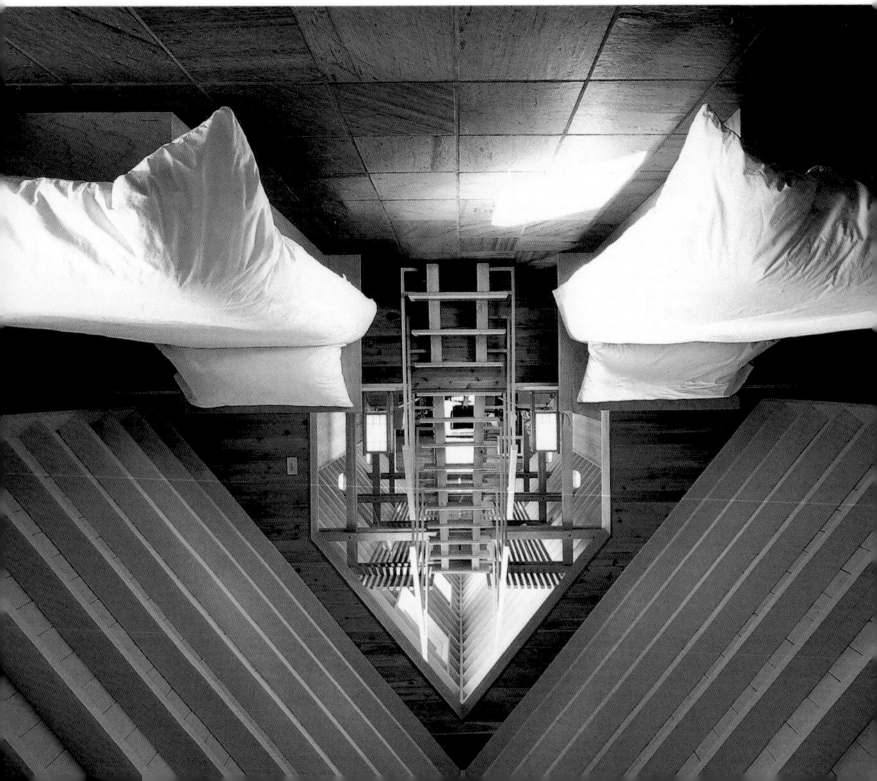

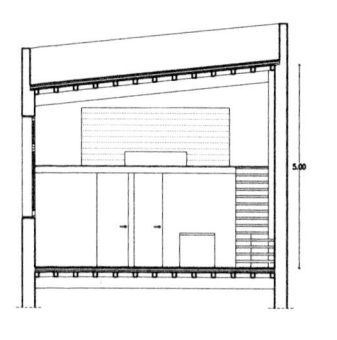

5.00

© Hiroyuki Hirai (3 photos)

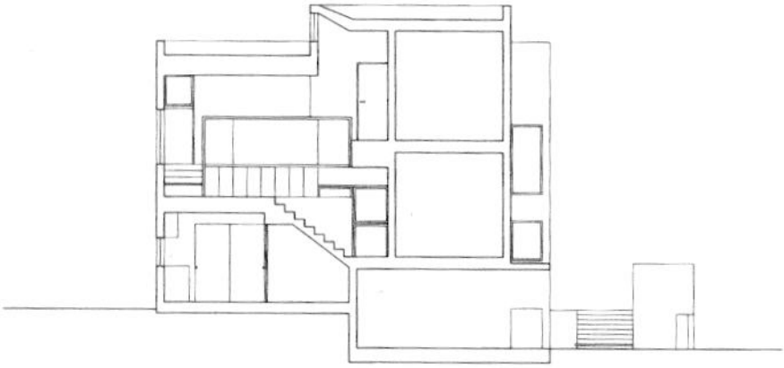

© Hiroyuki Hirai (2 photos)

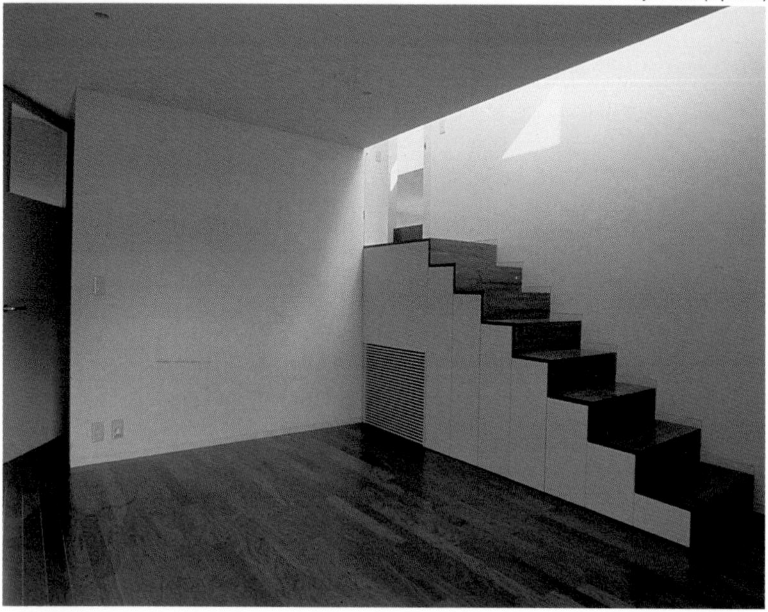

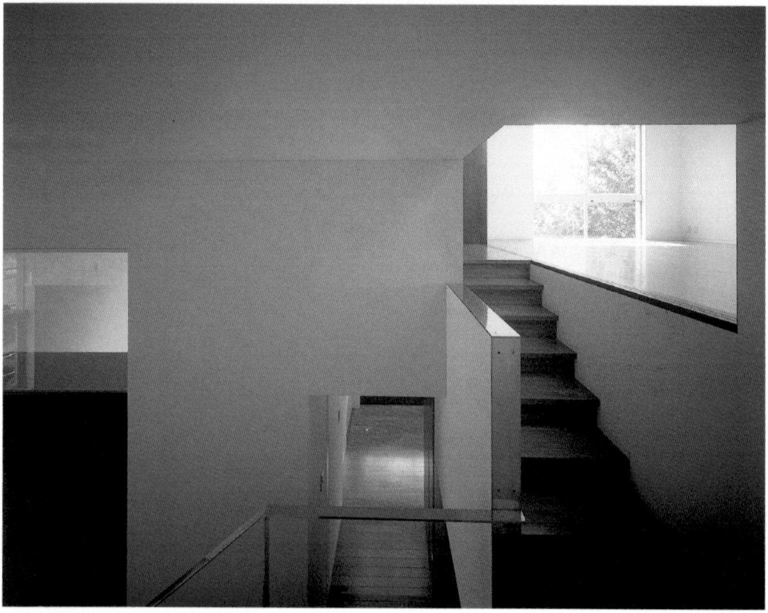

Using the same material on the floor and the staircase helps to integrate the latter into the space and unify the different levels.

Die Verwendung des gleichen Materials für den Boden und den Belag der Treppe trägt dazu bei, sie in den Raum zu integrieren und die Ebenen zu vereinheitlichen.

Recourir au même matériau pour le sol que pour l'escalier permet d'intégrer celui-ci dans l'espace et d'unifier les niveaux.

Usar el mismo material el pavimento en la escalera ayuda a incorporarla al espacio y a unificar los niveles.

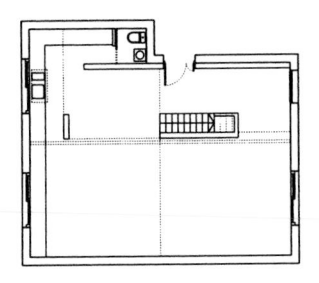
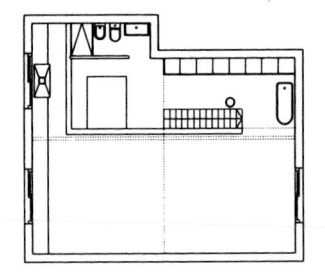

© Patricia Montalbetti

© Joan Mundó (2 photos)

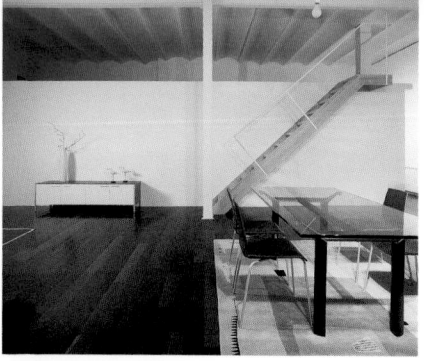

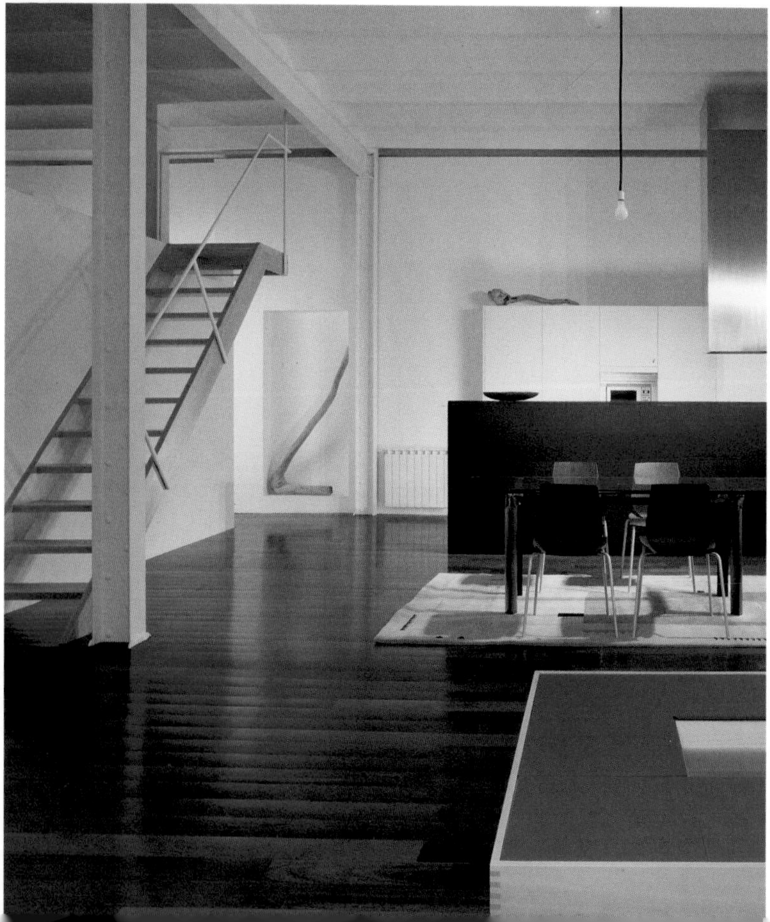

154

© Jordi Miralles (2 photos)

Concrete staircases
Betontreppen
Escaliers en béton
Escaleras de hormigón

Reinforced concrete is a relatively new material, but it has been extensively used ever since its appearance at the beginning of the twentieth century.

In order to make staircases, the concrete is first poured into a mold, made of wood, metal or plastic, in which it is left to harden. In order to make the material more resistant, metal reinforcements are inserted beforehand. Concrete staircases can also be prefabricated, either partially or totally.

Concrete is a long-lasting material that withstands traction and compression, but there is a danger of the metal reinforcement rusting, and so it is important that the building process is undertaken by experts. The durability of the material makes concrete staircases ideally suited to exteriors. Another great advantage is its resistance to fire.

The characteristics of concrete make it possible to build staircases in all shapes and sizes, with a less bulky appearance than those made of stone. However, in a domestic setting it must be remembered that the structure will be far heavier than a metal or wooden staircase.

The natural color of concrete is usually left unaltered, but it can be modified by adding minerals before it sets, or painting it once it is dry. It can also be clad with a wide range of materials: wood, metal, plaster, stone, ceramics, etc.

The construction details, such as handrails and treads, are generally made with other materials and their design can totally transform the appearance of a staircase.

Stahlbeton ist ein relativ junges Material, das seit seiner Einführung zu Beginn des 20. Jahrhunderts sehr viel verwendet wird.

Zur Herstellung von Treppen wird der Beton zur Aushärtung in Holz-, Metall- oder Plastikverschalungen gegossen. Zuvor werden Metallverstärkungen eingeführt, um die Haltbarkeit des Materials zu erhöhen. Betontreppen können teilweise oder komplett vorgefertigt werden.

Es ist ein sehr haltbares, gegen Zug und Druck beständiges Material. Es besteht jedoch die Gefahr, dass das eingelegte Metall rostet. Es ist daher wichtig, das der Konstruktionsprozess von Fachleuten durchgeführt wird. Betontreppen sind wegen ihrer Unverwüstlichkeit für den Außenbereich gut geeignet. Ein weiterer Vorteil ist ihre Feuerbeständigkeit.

Dank der Eigenschaften des Materials können die Treppen in den verschiedensten Formen ausgeführt werden und sie wirken leichter als Steintreppen. Bei ihrer Verwendung in Wohnungen muss ihr beachtliches Gewicht berücksichtigt werden. Im allgemeinen wird die natürliche Tönung des Betons beibehalten, selbst wenn man der Substanz Minerale beimischen oder in trockenem Zustand Farbe auftragen kann. Auch Verkleidungen mit vielen anderen Materialien sind möglich, z.B. mit Holz, Metall, Gips, Keramik... Details wie Handläufe oder Trittflächen werden für gewöhnlich in anderen Materialien ausgeführt, deren Auswahl und Design den Eindruck der Treppe vollkommen verändern können.

Le béton armé est un matériau relativement jeune mais a connu un réel essor depuis sa conception, aux débuts du XXème siècle.

La construction d'escaliers implique la réalisation d'un coffrage en bois, en métal ou en plastique, accueillant la coulée de béton pour qu'elle durcisse. Afin de le rendre plus résistant, des armatures de métal sont introduites au préalable. Les escaliers de béton peuvent également être préfabriqués en tout ou partie.

Il s'agit d'un matériau pérenne qui travaille bien en traction et en compression. Pour autant, persiste le risque d'oxydation de la structure métallique. De ce fait la construction doit être réservée aux professionnels. Les escaliers en bétons sont idéaux pour l'extérieur de par leur longévité. Un autre avantage conséquent : leur résistance au feu.

Ces caractéristiques permettent de créer des escaliers de forme et d'aspect très divers, plus légers que ceux constitués en pierre. Pour les maisons particulières, il est nécessaire de garder à l'esprit le poids considérable de la structure en regard des escaliers métalliques ou de bois.

Généralement, la couleur naturelle du béton est préservée, bien qu'il soit loisible de la faire varier en lui incorporant des minéraux ou en le peignant une fois sec. Il peut également être habillé : de bois, de métal, de ciment, de céramique...

Les détails de construction, mains courantes ou échelons, sont normalement d'un autre matériau, dont le choix et le design peuvent métamorphoser l'escalier.

El hormigón armado es un material relativamente joven, pero muy utilizado desde su concepción, a principios del siglo XX.

Para la construcción de escaleras, se vierte el hormigón en un encofrado de madera, metal o plástico en el que el material se endurece. Para que el material sea más resistente, se introducen previamente armaduras metálicas. Las escaleras de hormigón también pueden ser prefabricadas por partes o enteras.

Es un material duradero que trabaja bien a tracción y a compresión. Sin embargo, existe el peligro de que la armadura metálica se oxide, por lo que es importante que el proceso constructivo se lleve a cabo por profesionales. Las escaleras de hormigón son idóneas en el exterior por su durabilidad. Otra de sus grandes ventajas es la resistencia al fuego.

Gracias a las características del material se pueden realizar escaleras de muy diversas formas y de aspecto más ligero que las de piedra. Para su uso en viviendas se debe tener en cuenta que la estructura tendrá un peso considerable en comparación con escaleras metálicas o de madera. Por lo general, se mantiene el color natural del hormigón, aunque se puede variar añadiendo minerales a su composición o pintándolo cuando está seco. También se puede revestir con numerosos materiales: madera, metal, yeso, cerámica...

Los pasamanos o las huellas se suelen realizar en otros materiales, cuya elección y diseño pueden cambiar por completo el aspecto de la escalera.

© Eugeni Pons

© Christian Richters

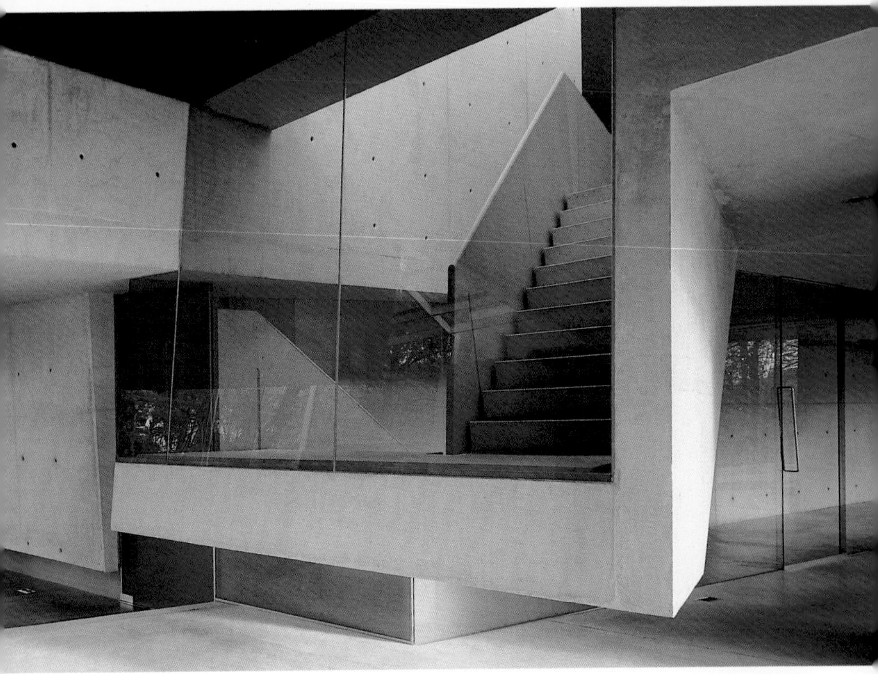

© Eduard Hueber

Despite their solidity, concrete staircases can look very light, even when they are used outdoors.

Trotz ihrer soliden Beschaffenheit können sogar für Außenanlagen sehr schwerelos wirkende Betontreppen entworfen werden.

En dépit d'une matérialité pesante, il est envisageable de concevoir des escaliers en béton d'aspect léger, même pour un usage extérieur.

A pesar de su materialidad sólida se pueden diseñar escaleras de hormigón de aspecto muy ligero, incluso para uso exterior.

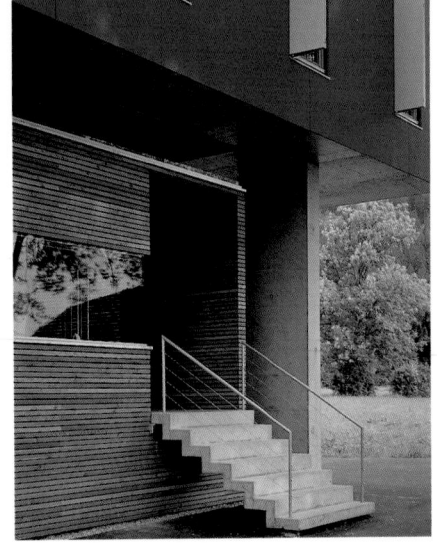

The patio in this urban house boasts a staircase with two different elements, both made of concrete: the first flight consists of three chunky steps, while the delicate lines of the second, stripped of banisters, follow the contours of the wall.

Vom Hof dieser Stadtwohnung geht man über eine Treppe aus verschiedenen Betonelementen nach oben: Der erste Abschnitt besteht aus drei massiven Stufen während sich der zweite Teil mit feinen Profilen und geländerlos an der Mauer hinaufzieht.

Depuis le patio de cette demeure urbaine s'élance un escalier constitué de différents éléments de béton : la première volée comporte trois échelons massifs, la seconde est dépourvue de main courante et grimpe le long du mur par de fins profils.

Desde el patio de esta vivienda urbana se sube por una escalera compuesta por diferentes elementos de hormigón: el primer tramo está formado por tres escalones macizos mientras el segundo sube a lo largo de la pared con perfiles finos y sin barandilla.

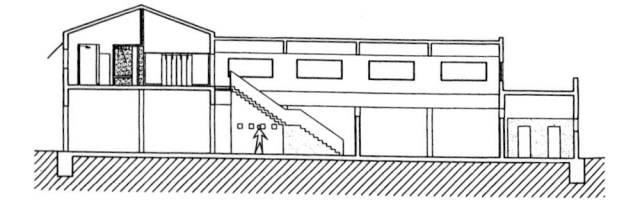

© Pere Planells (4 photos)

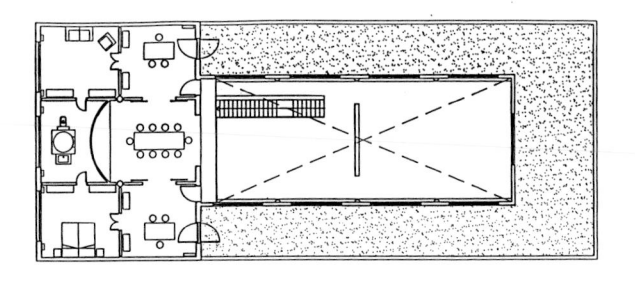

© Gregori Civera

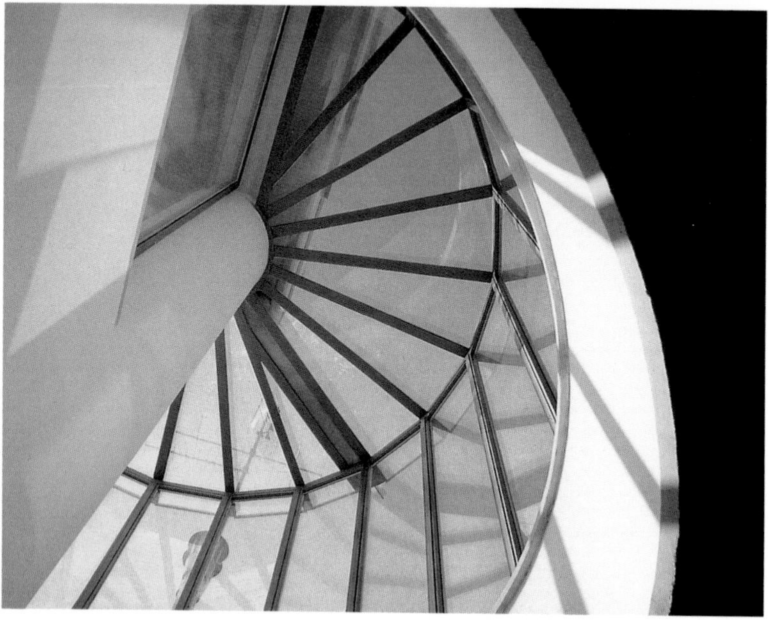

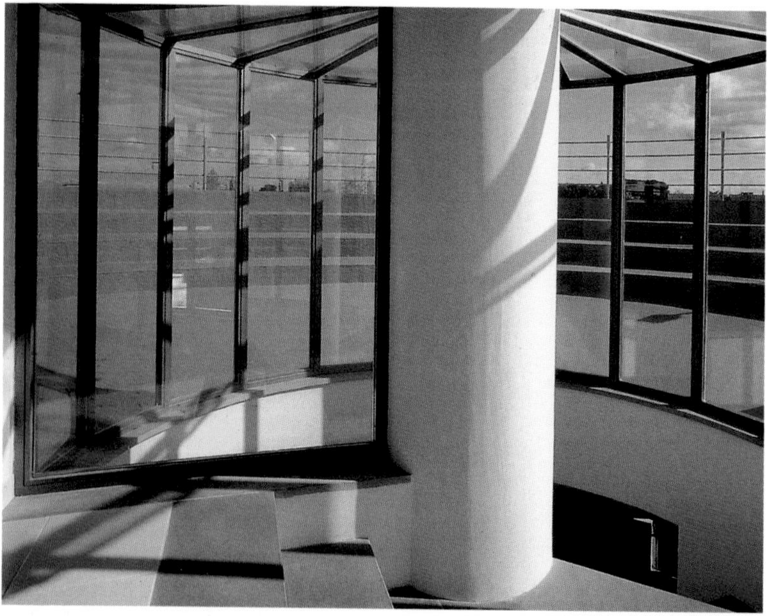

© Luis Gordoa (3 photos)

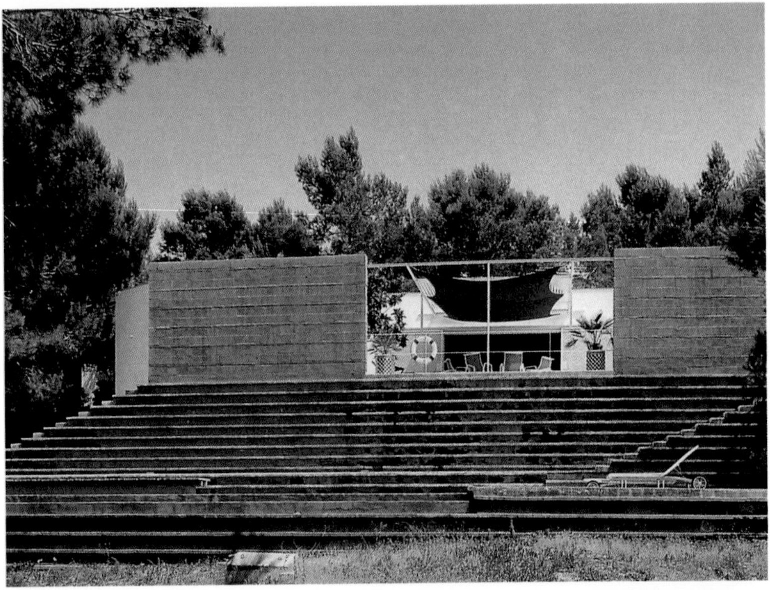

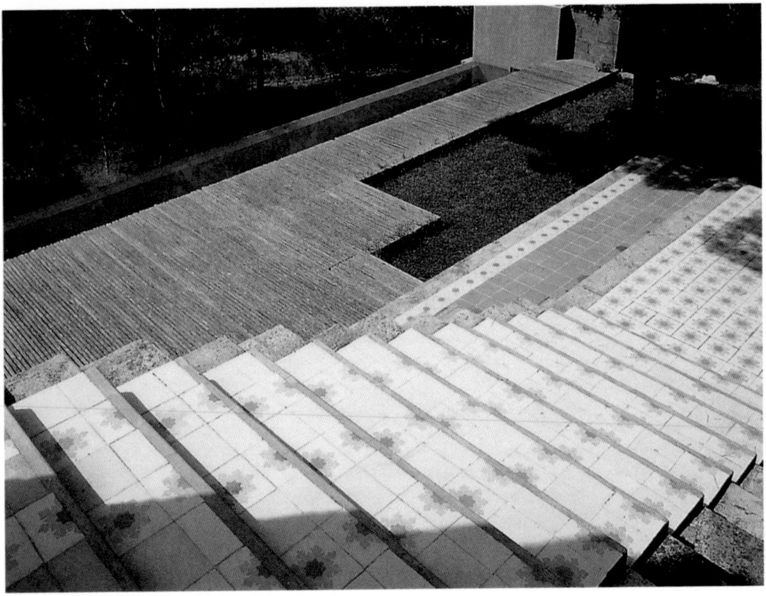

The reinforced concrete structure of this staircase in a public building is clad with stone sheets identical to those on the floor.

Eine Verkleidung mit den gleichen Steinplatten wie der Fußbodenbelag überdeckt die Stahlbetonstruktur dieser Treppe in einem öffentlichen Gebäude.

Le revêtement de plaques de pierre, identiques à celles du sol, se superpose à la structure en béton armé qui compose cet escalier d'un bâtiment public.

El revestimiento de placas de piedra, las mismas que en el suelo, se superpone a la estructura de hormigón armado que compone esta escalera en un edificio público.

© Jordi Miralles (3 fotos)

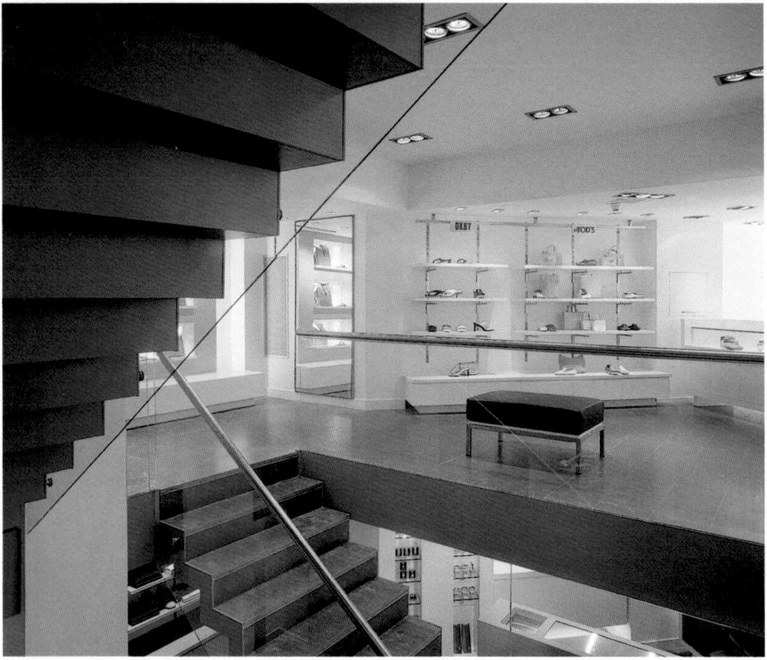

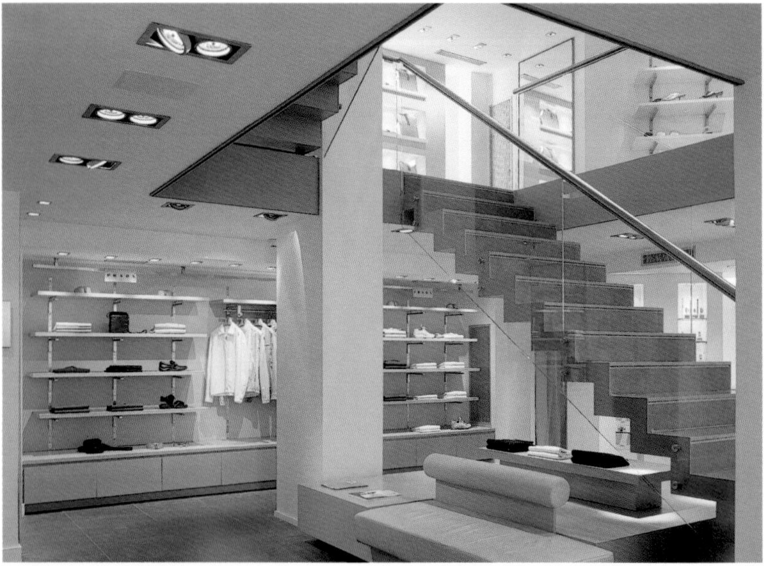

© Behnisch & Partner

Stone and brick staircases
Stein- und Ziegeltreppen
Escaliers en pierre et brique
Escaleras de piedra y ladrillo

Stone was one of the very first building materials. As it is heavy and difficult to transport, in the past only stones from a quarry near the construction site were used. These days it has come to be appreciated once again for its natural appearance and, if a budget allows, stones can be specially imported from all corners of the globe.

In former times stone staircases gave an imposing, regal air to palaces, temples and churches, but nowadays contemporary architects and designers are mainly drawn to stone because it ages so well and takes on a wide variety of patinas.

Stone, whether natural or artificial, is the material par excellence for use in outdoor settings. Its resistance and minimal maintenance requirements also make it ideally suited to staircases in public buildings and residential blocks. Anti-slip materials are generally applied to the treads to avert the danger of sliding.

It can also be used inside family houses, where it is normally combined with other materials to lighten the structure of a staircase and endow it with a more homely appearance. Stone blends in well with metals and other materials, especially those with smooth surfaces.

Another material that is often used in staircases is brick; this provides constructional qualities similar to those of stone, but it is easier to handle and cheaper to produce. However, in recent years both these materials have been superseded by reinforced concrete and metal structures.

Stein gehört zu den ältesten Baustoffen. Da es sich um ein schweres und schwierig zu transportierendes Baumaterial handelt, wurden in der Vergangenheit nur Steine aus Steinbrüchen in der Nähe der Baustelle verarbeitet. Heute hat seine natürliche Beschaffenheit wieder an Wert gewonnen und es werden Steine aus aller Welt verwendet, sofern das Budget es erlaubt.

Früher verliehen die Steintreppen den Palästen, Tempeln und Kirchen ein majestätisches Aussehen, während die modernen Architekten heute das Material wegen seiner guten Alterungseigenschaften und der vielfältigen Patina schätzen.

Natursteine oder künstliche Steine eignen sich par excellence für ihre Verwendung im Freien. Wegen ihrer Haltbarkeit und geringen Wartung sind sie ideal für Treppen in öffentlichen Gebäuden oder in Wohnblöcken. Um die Rutschgefahr zu verhindern, werden rutschfeste Materialien in die Trittfläche eingelegt.

In Einfamilienhäusern kommen sie ebenfalls zur Anwendung; dort werden sie meistens mit anderen Materialien kombiniert, um die Treppenstruktur leichter zu gestalten und ihr Wärme zu verleihen. Stein verträgt sich gut mit Metallen und anderen glattflächigen Materialien.

Ein weiteres, sehr häufig verwendetes Material ist Ziegel, dessen Konstruktionseigenschaften dem Stein ähnlich, dessen Herstellung und Bearbeitung aber leichter und wirtschaftlicher sind. Beide Materialien wurden in den letzten Jahren in vielen Fällen durch Stahlbeton oder Metallstrukturen ersetzt.

La pierre : un des premiers matériaux de construction. Autrefois son poids et les difficultés de transport inhérentes réservaient l'utilisation des pierres aux œuvres proches de leur carrière. Son aspect naturel est de nouveau au goût du jour et, si le budget le permet, il est loisible d'employer des pierres des quatre coins du globe.

Auparavant, les escaliers de pierre apportaient une majesté grandiose aux palais, temples et églises. Actuellement, ce sont plutôt leurs excellentes capacités de vieillissement et de patines très diverses que les architectes et designers apprécient. La pierre, naturelle ou artificielle, est le matériau d'extérieur par excellence. Sa résistance et son entretien facile la rendent également idéale pour les escaliers des édifices publics ou d'immeubles particuliers. Pour éviter les risques de glissade, des matériaux anti-dérapants sont appliqués sur les marches.

On la retrouve aussi dans les maisons particulières, où elle est habituellement associée à d'autres matériaux pour alléger la structure de l'escalier et lui conférer une touche chaleureuse. La pierre se marie bien avec les métaux ou autres matériaux, spécialement les surfaces lisses.

La brique est un autre matériau fréquemment employé, offrant des prestations de constructions semblables à celle de la pierre, bien que de production et d'élaboration plus simples et économiques. Pour autant, les deux matériaux se sont vus remplacés ces dernières années par le béton armé ou les structures métalliques.

La piedra fue uno de los primeros materiales de construcción. Por ser un elemento pesado y difícil de transportar, en el pasado se utilizaban sólo piedras de canteras cercanas a la obra. Hoy en día se valora nuevamente su aspecto natural y si el presupuesto lo permite, se llegan a emplean piedras de cualquier parte del mundo.

Antiguamente las escaleras de piedra aportaban una gran majestuosidad a palacios, templos e iglesias. Mientras que en la actualidad, los arquitectos y diseñadores contemporáneos aprecian el material porque envejece muy bien y llega a adquirir pátinas muy variadas.

La piedra natural o artificial es el material por excelencia para el uso exterior. Por su resistencia y fácil mantenimiento es también idóneo para escaleras en edificios públicos o bloques de viviendas. Para evitar el riesgo de resbalar, se aplican materiales antideslizantes en las huellas. Se utiliza también en viviendas unifamiliares, donde acostumbra a combinarse con otros materiales para aligerar la estructura de la escalera y dotarla de un aspecto más cálido. La piedra combina bien con los metales u otros materiales, especialmente de superficies lisas.

Otro material utilizado con gran frecuencia es el ladrillo, que ofrece prestaciones constructivas parecidas a la piedra, aunque su producción y elaboración son más fáciles y económicas. Sin embargo, ambos materiales se han sustituido en estos últimos años por el hormigón armado o las estructuras metálicas.

© Miquel Tres

The stone staircases in parks and public buildings are often used to create benches and bleachers.
A colored painting on the steps lightens the severity of this staircase providing access to a university in the USA.

Steintreppen in Parks oder öffentlichen Gebäuden dienen häufig zur Schaffung von Bänken und Tribünen.
Eine Farbzeichnung auf den Stufen lockert die Ernsthaftigkeit der Zugangstreppe zu einer Universität in den USA auf.

Les escaliers de pierre des parcs ou édifices publics sont très souvent détournés pour créer des bancs, voire des tribunes.
Un dessin de couleur sur les marches rompt l'austérité de l'escalier offrant accès à une université américaine.

Las escaleras de piedra en parques o edificios públicos se aprovechan en muchas ocasiones para crear bancos y tribunas.
Un dibujo en color en los peldaños rompe la seriedad de la escalera que da acceso a una universidad en EE.UU.

These stone staircases in up-market fashion stores boast a finishing of great purity. A coat of black lacquer, of varying width, accentuates the elegant dignity of the staircase on the right.

Diese Steintreppen in teuren Mode-Boutiquen zeigen eine bemerkenswerte Stilreinheit. Eine schwarze, unterschiedlich breite Lackschicht auf Teilen des Laufes hebt die Eleganz der rechten Treppe hervor.

Ces escaliers de pierre des boutiques de mode de luxe affichent une finition d'une grande pureté. Une couche de laque noire, de largeur variable sur certaines volées, accentue la noblesse de l'escalier de droite.

Estas escaleras de piedra en tiendas de moda de alta gama muestran un acabado de gran pureza. Una capa de laca negra, de ancho variable en parte de los tramos, acentúa la nobleza de la escalera a la derecha.

© Hertha Hurnaus (4 photos)

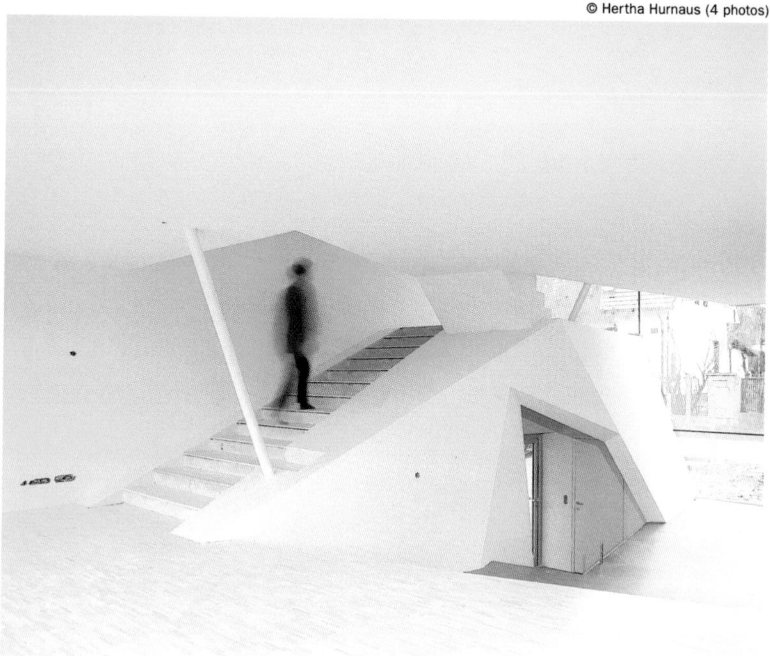

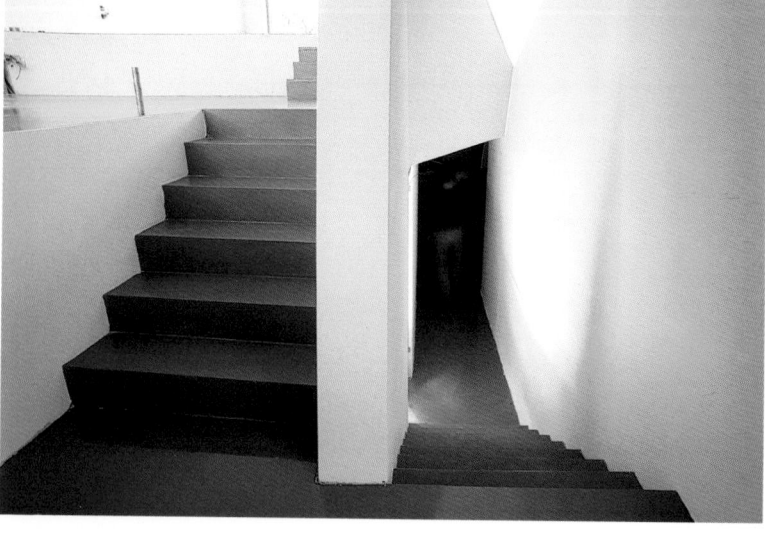

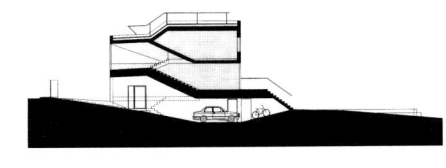

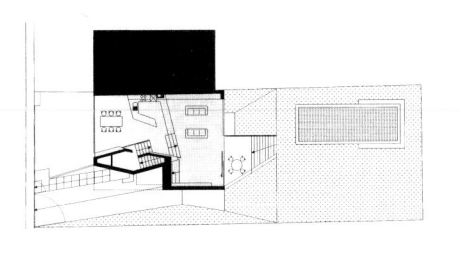

Aiming high can require for an unusual staircase, like this one leading to a bathtub.

Das Ziel, höhere Ebenen zu erreichen, kann zur Konzeption dieser überraschenden Treppe als Zugang zu einer Badewanne führen.

L'objectif d'atteindre des niveaux plus élevés peut amener à concevoir un étrange escalier permettant d'accéder...à une baignoire.

El objetivo de alcanzar niveles más altos puede llevar a concebir una curiosa escalera para acceder a una bañera.

© Studio Azzurro (2 fotos)

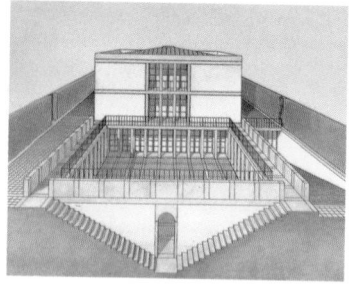

© Miquel Tres

© Undine Pröhl (3 photos)

© Luis Ferreira Alves (2 photos)

The robustness of stone can be alleviated by modern details, such as the pure lines of this transparent glass banister.

Der massive Eindruck des Natursteins kann mit einem modernen Detail aufgelockert werden, wie z. B. durch dieses durchscheinende Geländer reiner Linien.

Le caractère massif de la pierre peut être nuancé avec un détail moderne comme cette main courante en verre translucide, aux lignes pures.

La robustez de la piedra se puede aligerar con un detalle moderno como es esta barandilla de vidrio traslucido de líneas puras.

© Eugeni Pons (3 photos)

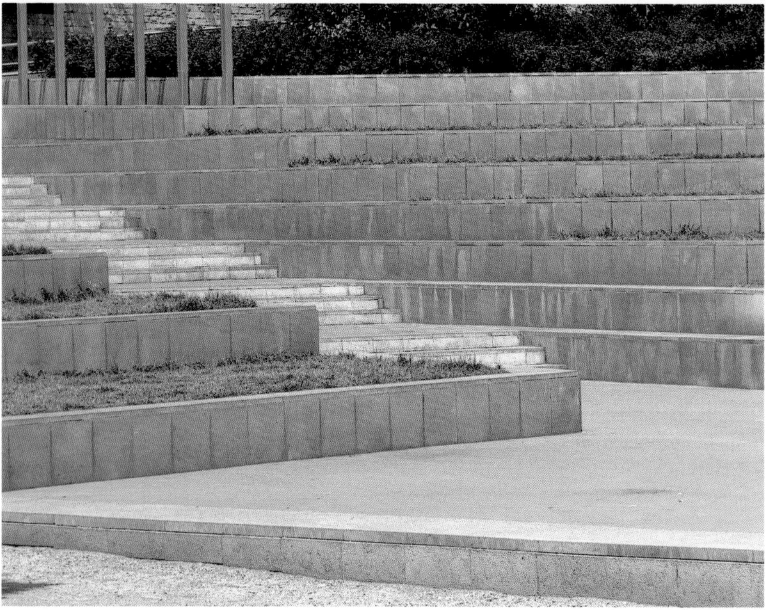

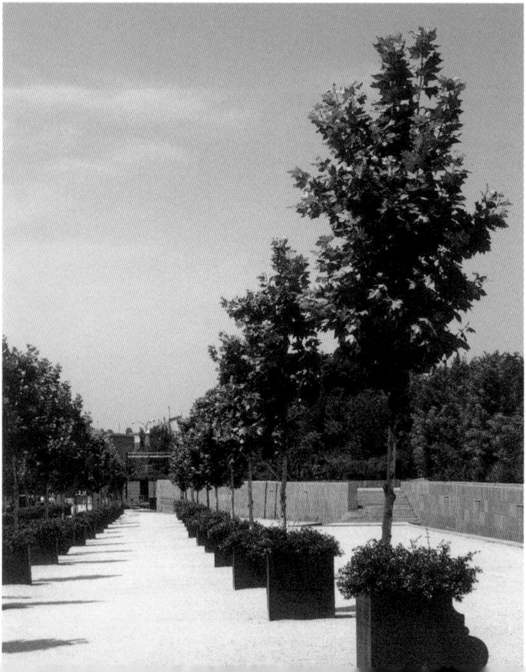

An original detail like a thin column under the landing can bestow elegance on a staircase while allowing it to satisfy all the regulations for a public building – in this case, a school.

Das originelle Detail in Form einer dünnen Säule unter dem Absatz verleiht dieser Treppe in einer Schule einen Hauch von Eleganz und erfüllt andererseits alle Vorschriften für ein öffentliches Gebäude.

Un détail original pour un délicat pilier sous le palier est à même de conférer une certaine élégance à un escalier qui, par ailleurs, répond à toutes les normes des constructions publiques, comme dans cette école.

Un detalle original como un fino pilar debajo del descanso puede dar elegancia a una escalera que, por otra parte, cumple todas las normas para un edificio público como esta en una escuela.

Glass staircases
Glastreppen
Escaliers en verre
Escaleras de vidrio

Glass is a material that was not traditionally used in the construction of staircases. However, it is a fascinating element that has a unique advantage: its transparency. The flights, landings or steps of a staircase made with glass allow light to pass through, and for this reason they are ideal for confined spaces and stories that receive little light, such as basements. It is not necessary to make a whole staircase out of glass. The same effect can be achieved just by applying the material to a single flight or a few steps, while the rest of the staircase can be built with more conventional materials.

Glass can be disconcerting in a staircase, due to its apparent fragility and lightness. Steps and banisters must always be built with special types of glass, such as wired glass, which contains small metal reinforcements that increase the material's resistance. It is also advisable to use safety glass, which does not splinter when broken into small pieces.

Glass staircases generally rely on a metal structure that serves as a frame for the steps and provides greater solidity and stability. This formula also solves the problem of making joints and fixing the glass to the walls and the staircase's support on the upper level. Staircases that are built entirely of glass do, however, have the disadvantage of being unstable. The transparency of the staircase, or of some of its details, can create plays of light – whether from natural or artificial sources – that can turn a staircase into an element imbued with a great visual richness.

Glas gehört nicht zu den traditionellen Konstruktionsmaterialien für Treppen. Es ist jedoch ein faszinierendes Material mit einem einzigartigen Vorteil: Transparenz. Die Läufe, Absätze oder Stufen aus Glas sind lichtdurchlässig und daher ideal für kleine Räume und Wohnungen mit wenig Licht, z.B. in Souterrains. Es ist nicht nötig, die gesamte Treppe in Glas auszuführen. Der gleiche Effekt kann mit nur einem Treppenlauf oder einigen Stufen aus Glas erreicht werden, während die restliche Treppe aus konventionelleren Materialien besteht.

Glas überrascht durch seine Zerbrechlichkeit und scheinbare Schwerelosigkeit. Für den Entwurf von Stufen oder Geländern darf nur Spezialglas mit eingearbeiteter Metallverstärkung zur Erhöhung der Haltbarkeit verwendet werden. Es wird empfohlen, Sicherheitsglas einzusetzen, das in kleine Stücke zerspringt, da so Schnittwunden vermieden werden.

Glastreppen sind normalerweise mit einer Metallstruktur versehen, die die Stufen umrahmt, um so größere Haltbarkeit und Stabilität zu erzielen. Auf diese Weise werden gleichzeitig die Probleme der Befestigung an den Mauern, der Fugen und der Auflage der Treppe an der Decke gelöst. Vollkommen in Glas ausgeführte Entwürfe haben den Nachteil geringerer Stabilität.

Die Transparenz der Treppe oder ihrer Details lässt Spiele mit natürlichem und künstlichem Licht zu, das die Treppen zu anregenden Elementen plastischen Reichtums werden lässt.

Le verre est un matériau ne reposant sur aucune tradition pour l'édification des escaliers. Pourtant, l'élément est fascinant de par sa caractéristique unique : la transparence. Les volées, paliers ou marches d'un escalier en verre laissent passer la lumière et sont, de ce fait, idéaux pour les espaces confinés et les étages peu éclairés, tels les semi sous-sols. Il n'est pas nécessaire que l'ensemble de l'escalier soit en verre. Cet effet peut être simplement obtenu en appliquant le matériau sur une volée ou sur quelques marches, le reste de l'escalier pouvant être construit avec des matériaux plus conventionnels.

Le verre surprend de par sa fragilité et son apparence légère. Pour la création des marches, ou de la main courante, seuls des verres spéciaux doivent être employés. Ainsi les verres armés incorporant de fines armatures métalliques qui augmentent sa résistance. Par surcroît, les verres de sécurité sont recommandés, évitant les coupures en se brisant en petits fragments.

Habituellement les escaliers de verre s'intègrent à une structure métallique qui encadre les marches, leur conférant solidité et stabilité. De plus, sont ainsi résolues les questions de fixation aux murs, de joints et d'intégration de l'escalier dans la pièce forgée. Les constructions réalisées entièrement en verre ont pour inconvénient leur instabilité. La transparence de l'escalier ou de ses détails permet les jeux de lumière, naturelle ou artificielle, qui convertissent les escaliers en des éléments d'une intense richesse plastique.

El vidrio es un material que no tiene una tradición constructiva en la fabricación de escaleras. Sin embargo, es un elemento fascinante que tiene una ventaja única: la transparencia. Los tramos, descansos o peldaños de una escalera construida en vidrio dejan pasar la luz, y por eso son idóneos para espacios reducidos y plantas con poca luz, como los semisótanos. No es necesario realizar toda la escalera en vidrio. Este mismo efecto se puede conseguir sólo con la aplicación del material en un tramo o en algunos peldaños, mientras que el resto de la escalera se puede construir en materiales más convencionales.

El vidrio sorprende por su fragilidad y ligereza aparente. Para la construcción de los peldaños o de las barandilla se han de usar únicamente vidrios especiales, como los armados, que incorporan pequeñas armaduras metálicas que aumentan la resistencia del material. Además se recomiendan los vidrios de seguridad, que evitan cortes al romperse en pequeños fragmentos.

Las escaleras de vidrio acostumbran a incorporar una estructura metálica que enmarca los peldaños para obtener más solidez y estabilidad. Además, de esta manera se soluciona el problema de la fijación a los muros, de las juntas y del soporte de la escalera en el forjado. Las construcciones que se realizan enteramente en vidrio tienen el inconveniente de la inestabilidad. La transparencia de la escalera o de sus detalles permite unos juegos de luz que convierte las escaleras en unos elementos sugerentes de una gran riqueza plástica.

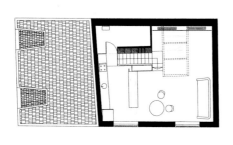

One of the undoubted advantages of a glass staircase is the fact that it allows light to penetrate into the space below. This effect is still achieved when only some of the steps are transparent and the others are built with more conventional materials.

Der unzweifelhafte Vorteil einer Glastreppe besteht in der Lichtdurchlässigkeit zu den darunter liegenden Räumlichkeiten. Der Effekt kann sogar mit nur wenigen transparenten Stufen erreicht werden, während der restliche Teil der Treppe mit konventionelleren Materialien ausgeführt wird.

Un avantage incontestable de l'escalier de verre : laisser la lumière se diffuser dans les espaces inférieurs. Cet effet peut être obtenu même lorsque seules les marches sont transparentes, alors que le reste de l'escalier est constitué de matériaux plus conventionnels.

Una indudable ventaja de la escalera de vidrio consiste en que deja pasar la luz a los espacios inferiores. Este efecto se consigue incluso con sólo unos peldaños transparentes mientras otra parte de la escalera se construye con materiales más convencionales.

© Fugitsuka Mitsumasa

Combinations of various materials
Kombination verschiedener Materialen
Combinaison de differents materiaux
Combinación de diferentes materiales

It is very common to find several materials combined in a single staircase, as this solution makes it possible to exploit all the advantages of the different materials. The choice of materials can give rise to a whole range of architectural styles and ways of bridging a gap between two levels.

The most frequent combinations involve wood and metal, reinforced concrete and metal or wood, or metal and wood. Some more delicate or very expensive materials – such as glass or fine woods or stones – are also almost always found in combination with other materials. One common strategy is the cladding of a solid structure with a more elegant and attractive material. Different materials can also be combined in the design of construction details, like the intersection with the banister or the joints between the steps.

The use of different materials can add harmony to a setting or, on the contrary, emphasize the contrasts between the various elements. The potential for combining materials knows no limits and makes it possible to give expression to a wide range of esthetic trends, resulting in original designs that can convert a functional feature into the highlight of a space.

However, combinations are not always just a question of esthetics. Combining material can be necessary for satisfying building regulations or for taking advantage of a preexisting structure. This is the case with renovations, where the application of new materials can serve to enhance the safety of the original staircase.

Im Treppenbau ist es üblich, Materialien zu kombinieren, um die verschiedenen Vorteile zu summieren. Je nach gewähltem Material ergeben sich vielfältige architektonische Stile, die in unterschiedlichsten Formen Niveauunterschiede überbrücken. Die häufigsten Kombinationen sind Holz und Metall, Stahlbeton und Holz oder Metall sowie Metall und Stein. Empfindlichere oder sehr kostspielige Materialien werden meist kombiniert, wie z. B. Glas, Edelhölzer oder teure Steine. Oft wird eine solide Struktur mit einem eleganteren und effektvolleren Material verkleidet. Auch werden Materialien beim Entwurf der Details kombiniert, wie z. B. für das Geländer oder die Fugen zwischen den Stufen.

Die Verwendung von verschiedenen Materialien dient einerseits zur harmonischen Gestaltung des Gesamtkomplexes und andererseits zur Betonung der Kontraste zwischen den verschiedenen Elementen. Den Möglichkeiten von Materialkombinationen sind keine Grenzen gesetzt. Sie können vielfältige ästhetische Tendenzen zum Ausdruck bringen sowie originelle Entwürfe schaffen, um ein funktionelles Element in den Mittelpunkt zu stellen.

Es dreht sich jedoch nicht immer um rein ästhetische Probleme. Die Kombination von Materialien kann infolge von konstruktiven Anforderungen unumgehbar werden, oder weil eine bestehende Struktur genutzt werden soll. Dies ist der Fall bei Umbauten, wo der Einsatz neuer Materialien dazu dienen kann, die Sicherheit der ursprünglichen Treppe zu erhöhen.

Il est d'usage d'associer divers matériaux lors de l'édification d'escaliers, leurs avantages respectifs pouvant se combiner. Selon les matériaux choisis, le résultat peut engendrer divers styles architecturaux et créer des formes variées de franchissement de niveaux.

Les combinaisons les plus usuelles allient le bois et le métal, le béton armé avec le métal ou le bois et enfin le métal et la pierre. Certains matériaux, plus délicats et très coûteux, sont essentiellement employés combinés à d'autres, comme par exemple le verre ou les pierres et essences nobles. Souvent, il s'agit d'habiller une structure solide avec un matériau plus élégant et vivant. De même, les matériaux se combinent lors de la conception de détails de construction, telle l'intersection avec la main courante ou les joints des marches.

L'utilisation de matériaux divers peut harmoniser l'ensemble ou, au contraire, mettre en avant les contrastes entre les différents éléments. Les possibilités de combinaison sont illimitées et permettent d'exprimer une vaste gamme de tendances esthétiques, créant des designs originaux pour offrir la vedette à un élément fonctionnel.

Mais parfois l'esthétique n'est pas tout. La combinaison de matériaux peut être nécessaire pour des impératifs de construction ou pour mettre à profit une structure existante. C'est le cas des rénovations, pour lesquelles l'application de nouveaux matériaux permet d'optimiser la sécurité de l'escalier original.

Es muy usual combinar varios materiales en la construcción de escaleras, porque se suman sus ventajas. Según los materiales elegidos, el resultado puede generar todo tipo de estilos arquitectónicos y conseguir variadas formas de salvar desniveles.

Las combinaciones más frecuentes son las que emparejan madera y metal, hormigón armado con metal o madera, metal y piedra. Algunos materiales más delicados o muy costosos suelen aparecer casi siempre en combinación con otros materiales, como p.ej. el vidrio o maderas o piedras nobles. En muchas ocasiones se trata de revestir una estructura sólida con un material más elegante y vistoso. También se combinan materiales al diseñar los detalles constructivos, como la barandilla o las juntas entre peldaños.

La utilización de distintos materiales puede armonizar el conjunto o, por el contrario, enfatizar los contrastes entre los diferentes elementos. Las posibilidades de combinaciones de materiales no tienen límites y permiten expresar una gran variedad de tendencias estéticas, creando diseños originales para convertir un elemento funcional en el protagonista del espacio.

Pero no siempre se trata de meras cuestiones de estética. La combinación de materiales puede ser necesaria por los requerimientos constructivos o porque se quiere aprovechar una estructura existente, p.ej. en las remodelaciones, donde la aplicación de nuevos materiales puede aumentar la seguridad de la escalera original.

© Studio Archea (3 photos)

This concrete structure with wooden cladding traces a winding path to the floor above. The steps on the upper reaches are deeper, to make the gradient smoother.

Diese Betonstruktur mit Holzverkleidung zeichnet einen gewundenen Weg in die obere Etage. Die Tiefe der oberen Stufen wurde erweitert und somit eine sanftere Neigung erreicht.

Cette structure en béton habillée de bois dessine un chemin sinueux vers l'étage supérieur. Les marches des dernières volées s'étendent en profondeur, offrant une pente plus douce.

Esta estructura de hormigón con un revestimiento de madera dibuja un camino sinuoso a la planta superior. Los peldaños de los últimos tramos se han extendido en profundidad, logrando una pendiente más suave.

© Francesc Tur (3 photos)

© Peter Hyatt (3 photos)

© Axel Sölvasson (2 photos)

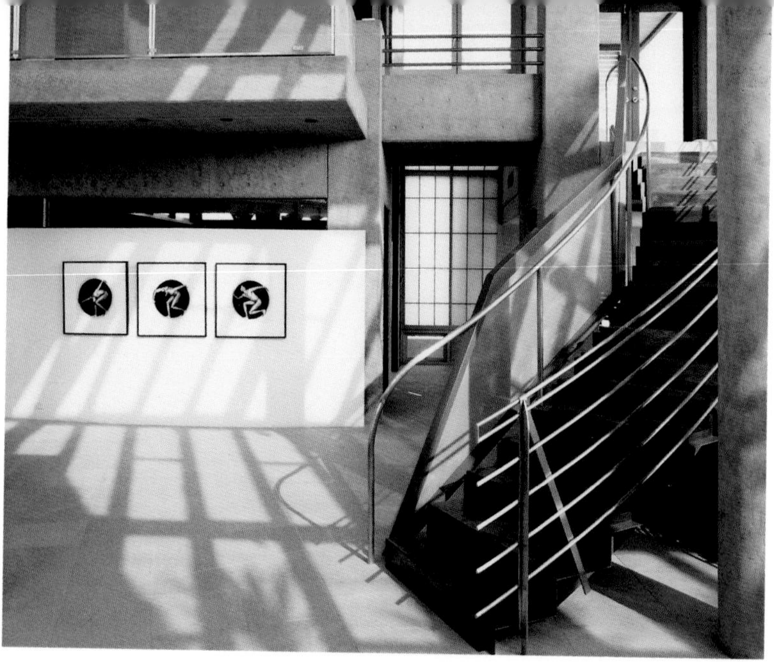

© Undine Pröhl (2 photos)

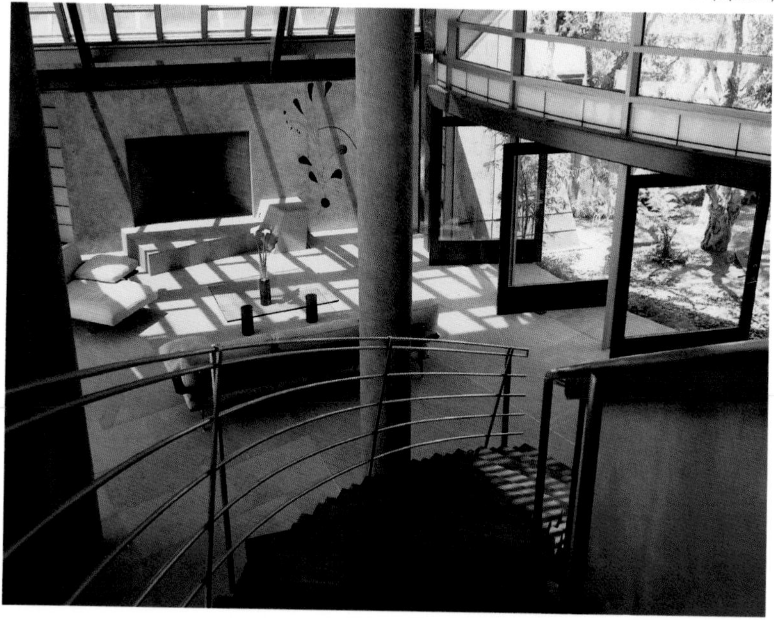

A strong contrast between
different materials can enrich
the whole staircase.

Der eindrucksvolle Kontrast
zwischen den verschiedenen
verwendeten Materialien
bereichert den Treppenkomplex.

Un fort contraste entre les
différents matériaux employés
enrichit l'ensemble de l'escalier.

Un fuerte contraste entre los
diferentes materiales utilizados
enriquece el conjunto de la
escalera.

Escalators and ramps
Rolltreppen und Rampen
Escaliers mécaniques et pentes
Escaleras mecánicas y rampas

The first escalator was unveiled to the world in 1900 at the Universal Exhibition in Paris. It was designed to transport people and goods in a short space of time without demanding any great exertion on the part of its users. Ever since then escalators have become common features of public buildings and, above all, shopping centers, where they have often completely replaced elevators, as they can hold a greater number of people at any one time.

In most cases the system comprises two parallel flights of stairs, one for going up and another for going down. As escalators take up a large amount of floor space, they are normally placed at central points in a building, thereby facilitating the flow of people. However, a conventional staircase must always be added, in case of an emergency. Safety requirements have led to very strict regulations for the construction of escalators, which particularly focus on the gradients, the characteristics of the handrails, the switches, the brakes and the emergency stops. Escalators are expensive to install and maintain and require specialist technical attention.

As for ramps, this system is particularly used in public buildings to facilitate the access of people with restricted mobility, as well as to allow the transportation of goods by means of wheeled conveyances. They often serve as a complement to a staircase. For safety reasons, the angle of a ramp's gradient must not exceed certain limits. It occupies a far greater floor space than a staircase and it is essential to cover it with anti-slip material.

Die erste Rolltreppe wurde 1900 auf der Weltausstellung in Paris vorgestellt. Das Ziel war, Menschen und Waren schnell und ohne große Anstrengung zu befördern. Seitdem wurden sie in erster Linie für öffentliche Gebäude und Geschäftszentren geplant, wo sie dank ihrer größeren Beförderungskapazität häufig die Aufzüge ersetzt haben.

Meistens besteht eine Rolltreppe aus zwei parallelen Läufen zum Hoch- und Hinunterfahren. Da sie viel Platz einnehmen, und um den Personen ihre Benutzung zu erleichtern, sind sie normalerweise zentral im Gebäude untergebracht. Für Notfälle muss jedoch immer eine konventionelle Treppe vorhanden sein. Die Sicherheitsanforderungen haben zu strengen Vorschriften für die Konstruktion geführt, die sich vor allem auf die Steigungswinkel, den Aufbau der Handläufe, auf Schalter, Bremsen und Not-Halt beziehen. Installierung und Wartung sind kostspielig und erfordern einen technischen Fachservice.

Rampen werden vor allen Dingen in öffentlichen Gebäuden verwendet, um Personen mit eingeschränkter Bewegungsfreiheit den Zugang sowie die Beförderung von Waren auf Rädern zu ermöglichen. Häufig werden sie ergänzend zur Treppe installiert. Die Neigung einer Rampe darf aus Sicherheitsgründen bestimmte Grenzwerte nicht übersteigen. Sie nimmt eine größere Fläche als eine Treppe ein und ihr Bodenbelag sollte aus rutschfestem Material sein.

Le premier escalier mécanique fut présenté lors de l'Exposition Universelle de Paris de 1900. Son objectif : déplacer personnes et marchandises en peu de temps et sans efforts. Depuis lors, leur usage s'est diffusé essentiellement dans les bâtiments publics et les espaces commerciaux, où ils ont souvent remplacé les ascenseurs, transportant plus de personnes simultanément.

Dans la plupart des cas le système comporte deux rampes parallèles, l'une pour monter et l'autre pour descendre. Gourmands en espace et devant faciliter la circulation des usagers, ils se situent essentiellement aux points centraux des édifices. Pour autant, un escalier conventionnel est toujours nécessaire en cas d'urgence. Les impératifs de sécurité ont engendré des règles très strictes pour leur construction, portant principalement sur la pente autorisée, les caractéristiques des mains courantes, les interrupteurs, les freins et les arrêts d'urgence. Leur installation et leur entretien sont coûteux et requièrent des services techniques spécialisés.

Quant aux rampes, il s'agit d'un système employé surtout dans les bâtiments publics pour faciliter l'accès des personnes à mobilité réduite mais permettant aussi le déplacement des marchandises sur roulettes. Elles existent souvent en complément d'un escalier. La pente d'une rampe ne doit pas dépasser certaines limites déterminées d'inclinaison, pour des motifs de sécurité. Elles requièrent une surface d'implantation supérieure à celle d'un escalier et leur parcours nécessite un revêtement anti-dérapant.

La primera escalera mecánica fue presentada en 1900 durante la Exposición Universal de París. El objetivo era desplazar a personas y mercancías en poco tiempo y sin mucho esfuerzo. Desde entonces, se han ido proyectando sobre todo en edificios públicos y espacios comerciales, donde en muchas ocasiones han sustituido a los ascensores, dado que transportan un mayor número de personas a la vez.

En la mayoría de los casos son dos tramos paralelos, uno para subir y otro para bajar. Al ocupar una gran superficie y para facilitar la circulación de los usuarios acostumbran a encontrase en puntos céntricos de los edificios. Sin embargo, siempre se necesita una escalera convencional para casos de emergencia. Los requerimientos de seguridad han llevado a una normativa muy estricta, que regula sobre todo los ángulos de subida, la construcción de los pasamanos, los interruptores, los frenos y las paradas de emergencia. La instalación y el mantenimiento son costosos y requieren servicios técnicos especializados.

En cuanto a las rampas, este sistema se utiliza sobre todo en los edificios públicos para facilitar el acceso a personas con movilidad limitada, al tiempo que permiten el desplazamiento de mercancías en soportes rodantes. Muchas veces son complementarias a una escalera. La pendiente de una rampa no debe sobrepasar unos determinados límites de inclinación por razones de seguridad. La superficie en la que se implanta es mayor a la de una escalera y su recorrido se ha de cubrir con material antideslizante.

© Jordi Miralles

286

© Undine Pröhl (3 photos)

One side of the wooden platform turns into the smooth slope of a ramp extending out over the indoor swimming pool, while the other side serves as an office.

Eine Galerie aus Holz teilt sich einerseits in die sanfte Neigung einer Rampe, die über den innenliegenden Pool führt, während die andere Seite zu einem Schreibtisch wird.

Une plate-forme de bois se divise, d'un côté, en la pente douce d'une rampe qui surplombe la piscine intérieure, l'autre partie se transformant en un bureau.

Una plataforma de madera se divide por un lado en la suave pendiente de una rampa que sobrepasa la piscina interior mientras el otro tramo se convierte en el escritorio.

© Ricardo Labougle

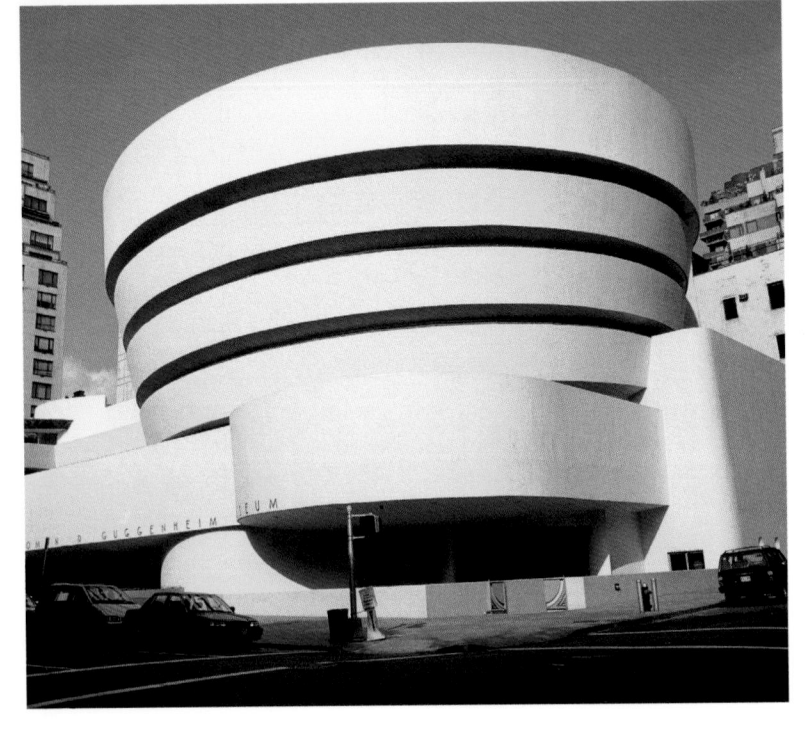

The use of ramps allows museums and galleries to create interesting and accessible layouts for their exhibitions.

Die Verwendung von Rampen in Museen und Ausstellungszentren bietet die Möglichkeit, interessante und angenehme Wege für die Besucher der Ausstellung zu schaffen.

L'emploi de rampes offre aux musées et centres d'exposition la possibilité de créer des parcours intéressants et progressifs pour visiter les expositions.

La utilización de rampas ofrece a los museos y centros de exposición la posibilidad de crear interesantes y suaves recorridos para visitar sus exposiciones.

Exterior staircases
Treppen im Freien
Escaliers à l'extérieur
Escaleras al exterior

Exterior staircases generally serve as access to a building. They usually consist of a single flight with only a few steps. Another use of exterior staircases can be seen in public spaces, such as gardens and squares, where they connect platforms or terraces with other levels. Sometimes staircases are combined with benches or bleachers, creating spaces that provide excellent vantage points for admiring the view below.

As exterior staircases are set in unconfined spaces they can take on large dimensions that endow them with an imperious quality; this often reinforces the social status a building is designed to project.

Exterior staircases are generally made of durable materials, as they have to endure the vicissitudes of the weather, such as rainfall and changes of temperature. However, it must be taken into account that, at temperatures below 0° C, water infiltrating a staircase can cause cracks in even the most resistant materials.

As a result of these determining factors, the most commonly used materials are stone, brick, reinforced concrete, iron and metal. A special finish is required in most cases, either to protect the structure or for purely esthetic reasons.

Another significant problem that has to be confronted is the risk of slipping on wet steps, especially if they have smooth surfaces like glass, marble and wood. It is therefore advisable to make steps out of rough materials or apply an anti-slip finish; so, metal steps usually incorporate a relief or grilles, while bands of anti-slip material are applied to stone.

Außentreppen werden im Allgemeinen als Zugang zu Gebäuden verwendet und sind normalerweise einläufig mit wenigen Stufen. Eine weitere Verwendung finden sie im öffentlichen Raum, in Parks oder auf Plätzen, wo sie verschiedene Ebenen miteinander verbinden. Gelegentlich werden sie mit Bänken oder Tribünen kombiniert und lassen so die privilegierte Betrachtung der Umgebung zu. Da sie in nahezu unbegrenztem Raum gebaut werden, sind ihre Dimensionen entsprechend groß und beeindruckend; dies vereint sich mit ihrer repräsentativen Aufgabe.

Die verwendeten Materialien sind in der Regel sehr haltbar, da sie Klimaschwankungen standhalten müssen, Feuchtigkeit ebenso wie Temperaturveränderungen. Bei Temperaturen unter 0° C muss jedoch berücksichtigt werden, dass eingesickertes Wasser selbst bei widerstandsfähigsten Materialien Risse verursachen kann.

Unter Berücksichtigung dieser Voraussetzungen werden am häufigsten Stein und Ziegel, Stahlbeton, Eisen und Stahl verwendet. In den meisten Fällen ist eine spezifische Behandlung erforderlich, sei es zum Schutz der Struktur oder aufgrund ästhetischer Kriterien.

Ein wichtiger zu berücksichtigender Faktor ist die Gefahr des Ausrutschens auf feuchten Stufen, besonders auf glatten Flächen wie Glas, Marmor oder Holz. Es werden daher rauhe Materialien empfohlen oder Materialien mit unebener oder rutschfester Oberfläche. Bei Metalltreppen bieten sich Gitter oder Reliefs an und bei Steintreppen eingelegte rutschfeste Streifen.

Les escaliers extérieurs permettent généralement d'accéder à un édifice. Ils comportent habituellement une seule volée et peu de marches. Ces escaliers permettent alternativement dans les espaces publics, comme les jardins ou les places, de connecter des plate-formes ou des terrasses à divers niveaux. Parfois ils se transforment en bancs ou en tribunes, créant des espaces offrant un point de vue privilégié sur l'environnement. Situés dans des espaces ouverts, ils peuvent adopter des dimensions plus amples, leur conférant une majesté qui se marie avec leur influence représentative.

Les matériaux de prédilection affectent une tendance à la pérennité, devant faire face aux outrages du temps, comme l'humidité et les changements de température. Pour autant, lorsque le thermomètre passe sous le zéro, il est nécessaire de prévoir les infiltrations d'eau susceptibles de fissurer les éléments les plus résistants.

Pour faire face à ces intempéries, les matériaux les plus utilisés sont la pierre et la brique, le béton armé, le fer et l'acier. Dans la plupart des cas, une finition spéciale est nécessaire que ce soit pour protéger la structure ou pour des critères essentiellement esthétiques. Il convient de garder présent à l'esprit un autre facteur important : le risque de glissade sur les marches humides, plus spécialement sur les surfaces lisses comme le verre, le marbre ou le bois. Pour cette raison, il est recommandé de recourir à des matériaux rugueux ou dotés d'une finition irrégulière ou anti-dérapante. Ainsi, les escaliers mécaniques intègrent des reliefs ou des grilles et la pierre se voit appliquée des bandes anti-dérapantes.

Las escaleras exteriores se utilizan en general como acceso al edificio. Acostumbran a ser de tramo recto y de pocos peldaños. Otro uso exterior de las escaleras se da en los espacios públicos, como jardines o plazas, en los que se conectan plataformas o terrazas a distinto nivel. A veces las escaleras se combinan con bancos o tribunas, creando espacios desde los que se puede apreciar el entorno de forma privilegiada. Al estar situadas en espacios no limitados llegan a adquirir grandes dimensiones, lo que les confiere majestuosidad, que se aúna con el carácter representativo que también ejercen.

Los materiales que se utilizan acostumbran a ser duraderos, ya que tienen que soportar las inclemencias del tiempo, como la humedad y los cambios de temperatura. Sin embargo, con temperaturas por debajo de 0° C, se ha de prever que el agua infiltrada puede fisurar los elementos más resistentes.

Los materiales más utilizados son la piedra y el ladrillo, el hormigón armado, el hierro y el acero. En la mayoría de los casos, se requiere un acabado específico, ya sea para proteger la estructura o por criterios meramente estéticos. Un factor importante que se ha de tener en cuenta es el riesgo de resbalar en los peldaños húmedos, especialmente en superficies lisas como el vidrio y el mármol on en la madera. Por eso para los escalones se recomiendan los materiales rugosos o con un acabado áspero o antideslizante. Así, las escaleras metálicas incorporan relieve o rejillas, y en la piedra se suele aplicar bandas antideslizantes.

© Michael Denancé & Georges Fessy

Fire escapes, so typical of the urban landscape in the USA, are often positioned on the exterior of a building and require the use of fire-resistant materials like metal.

Die für das Stadtbild in den USA so typischen Feuertreppen sind eine typische Form der Außentreppen und erfordern die Verwendung von feuerfesten Materialien, wie z. B. Metall.

Les escaliers d'incendie, si typiques des paysages urbains des Etats-Unis, sont fréquemment utilisés en extérieur et requièrent l'emploi de matériaux résistants au feu, tel le métal.

Las escaleras de incendio, tan típicas en el paisaje urbano de EE.UU., son una utilización frecuente al exterior y requieren el uso de materiales resistentes al fuego como el metal.

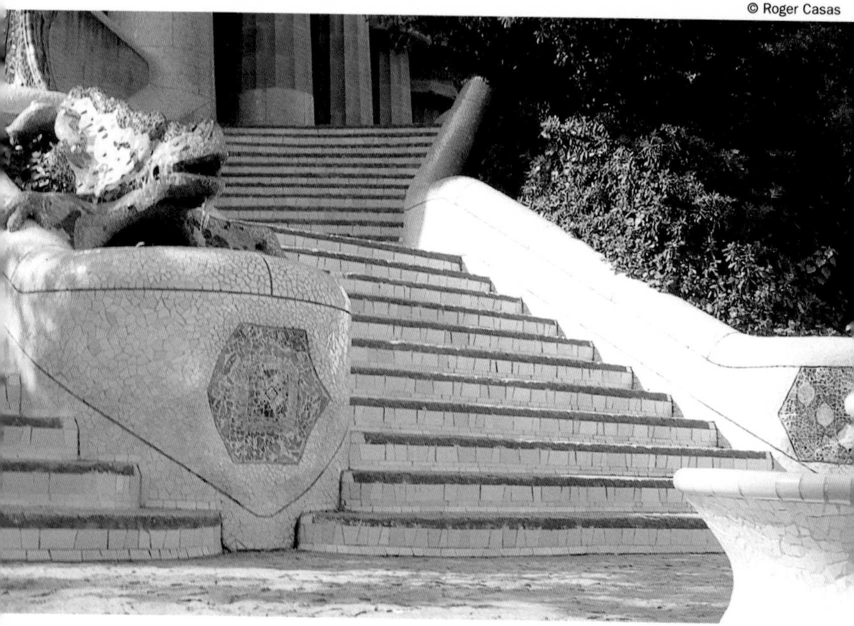

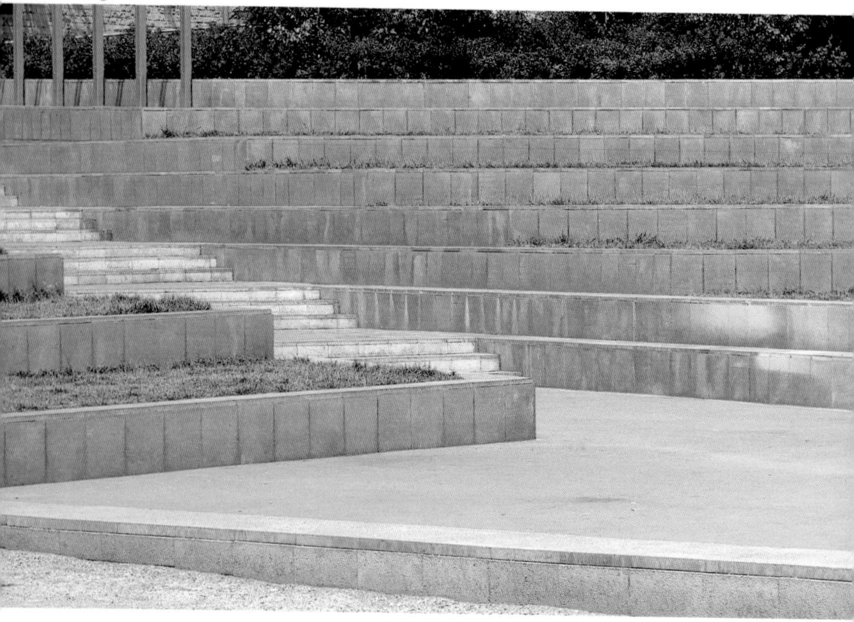

© Miquel Tres (2 photos)

© Stefan Müller (2 photos)

© Miquel Tres

A staircase can define a space or a landscape, whether on a small scale, as in a private garden, or as the dominant element in an architectural composition, as in this historic museum in Japan.

Eine Treppe kann einen Raum oder eine Landschaft definieren; auf kleiner Ebene wie in diesem Privatgarten oder als Hauptelement architektonischer Gestaltung wie in diesem historischen Museum in Japan.

Un escalier peut définir un espace, voire un paysage : pour un simple jardin particulier ou comme élément principal d'une composition architecturale ainsi dans ce musée d'Histoire au Japon.

Una escalera puede definir un espacio o un paisaje; a pequeño nivel como en un jardín particular o como principal elemento de composición arquitectónica como en este museo histórico en Japón.

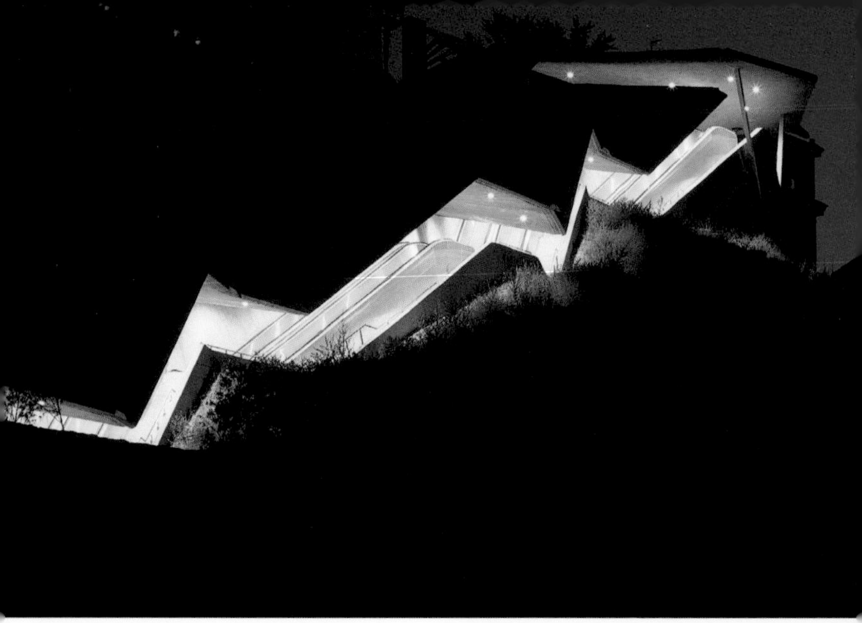

© David Cardelús (4 photos)

p. 312 © Toshiharu Kitahama
p. 313 © Eugeni Pons

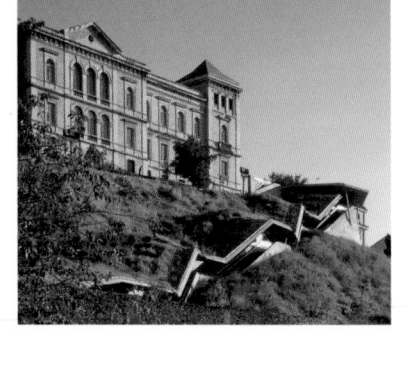

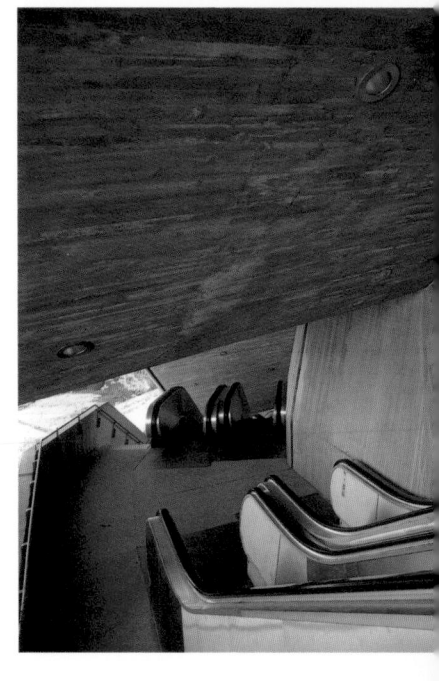

© Eduard Hueber (2 photos)

© Baumschlager & Eberle

© Eugeni Pons

© Koji Okamoto (2 photos)

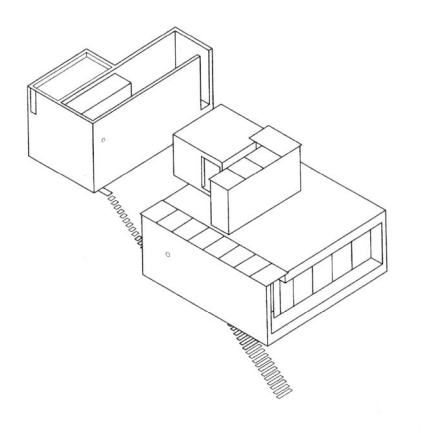

© Hertha Hurnaus

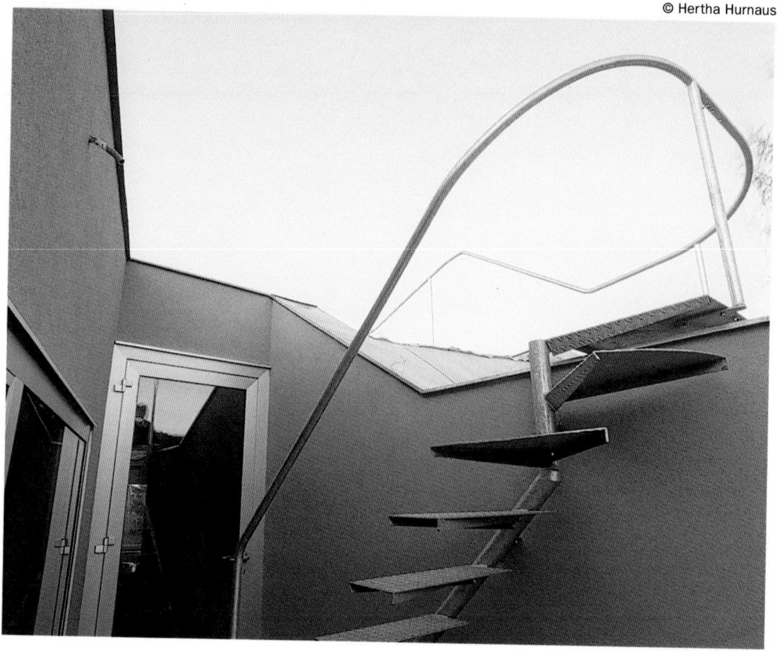

© Hiroyuki Hirai

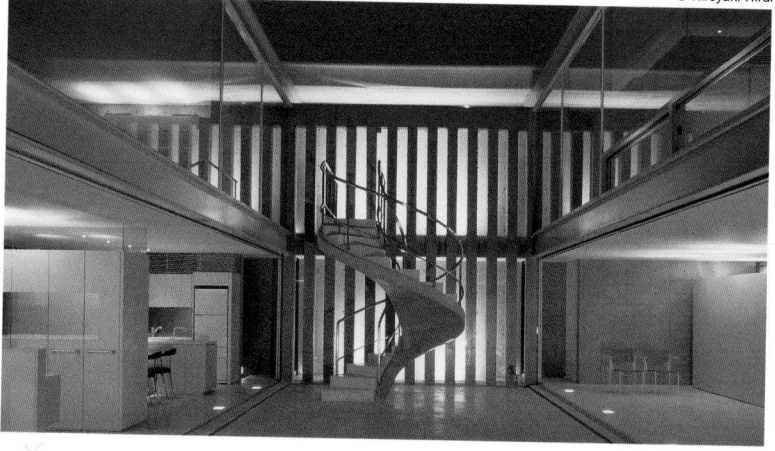

© Luc Svetchine (3 photos)

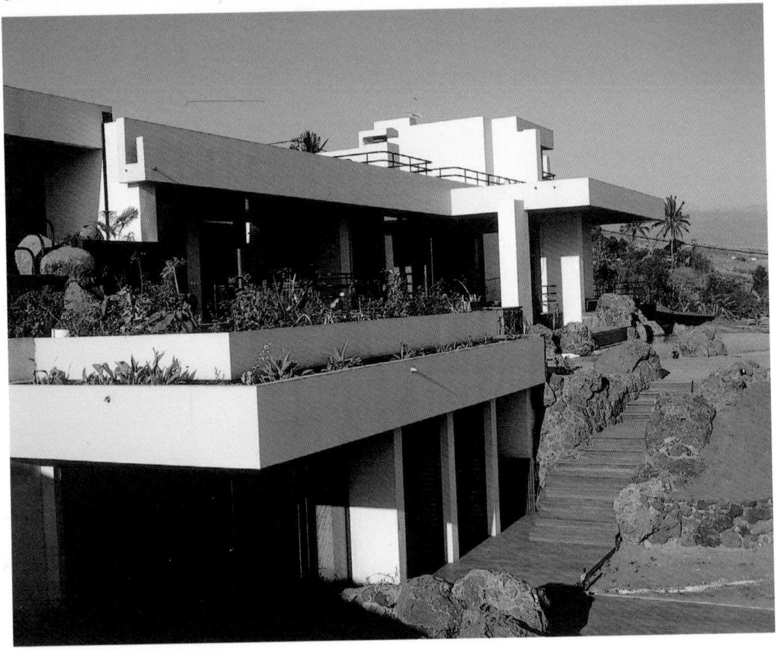

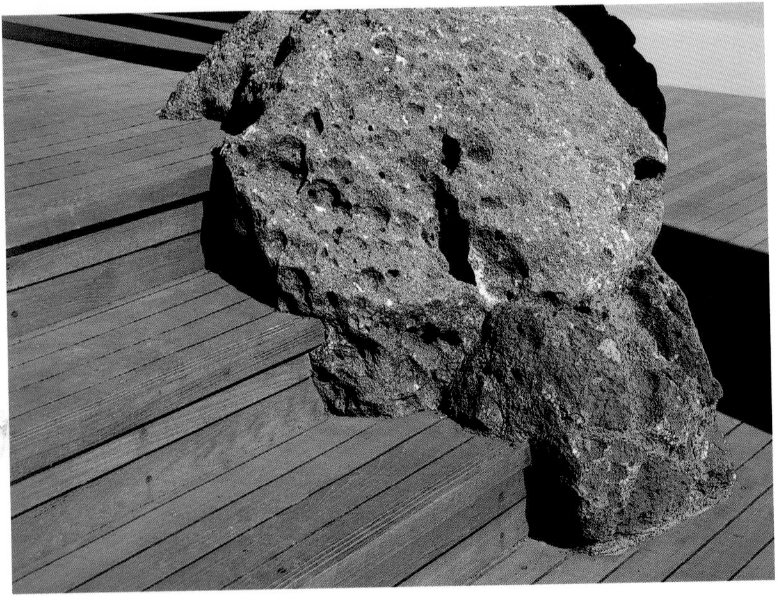

The need to link the different levels found within a city - such as those created by the installation of a canal - can be satisfied by means of striking steps that embellish the urban landscape.

Im Stadtbild müssen häufig Niveauunterschiede überbrückt werden, z. B. durch die Integrierung eines Kanals. Dies kann mit ausdrucksstarken Treppen gelöst werden, die die städtische Landschaft verschönern.

Des escaliers emblématiques, réinventant les paysage urbains, permettent de faire face aux dénivelés de la forme urbaine d'une cité, ainsi l'intégration d'un canal.

La necesidad de salvar los desniveles en la forma urbana de una ciudad, p. ej. por la integración de un canal, se puede solucionar mediante escaleras emblemáticas que embellecen el paisaje urbano.

© Tom Bonner

© Jean Marie Monthiers (3 photos)

Details

Details

Details

Detalles

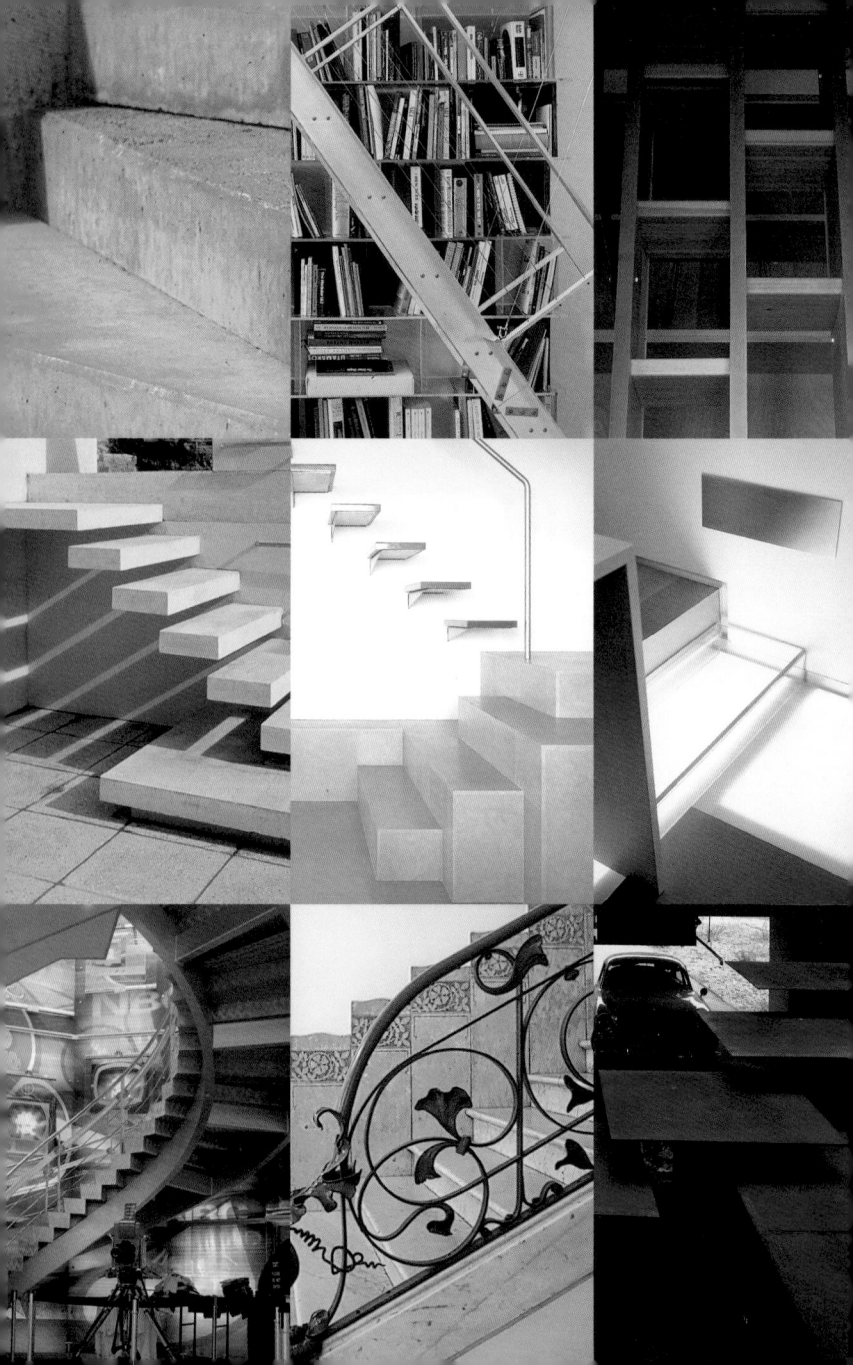

Steps
Stufen
Marches
Escalones

Several factors impinge on the design of a staircase and, when these are taken in combination, they can give rise to a wide range of solutions. The setting and use of a staircase, as well as personal tastes, also bear an influence on the end result. Similarly, all the features of steps are open to variation, even on a single staircase: form, dimension, materials, etc.

It is vital for a staircase to be well lit from top to bottom to ensure that it can be used safely. In the case of compensated staircases, the steps must overlap to provide sufficient space for the feet. However, it must be remembered that overlapping steps can cast a shadow on the treads below, thereby reducing their visibility. It is therefore advisable to design the treads and risers in different colors or mark the edges of the steps.

The design of the steps can also give a setting a distinctive look. One good example of this is steps made of robust blocks set directly into the wall, which leave a greater floor space available in the room below. Other strategies are the separation of the staircase from the wall – by less than an inch – to make the structure appear lighter, or the application of cladding or paintwork on just some of the steps.

In some cases the steps can also serve an independent function. So they can be used as a platform for decorative objects, as an integral part of bookshelves or as the support for a source of light.

Beim Design einer Treppe spielen verschiedene Faktoren zusammen, die untereinander kombiniert abwechslungsreiche Lösungen ergeben können. Der Raum, die Nutzung sowie der persönliche Geschmack nehmen Einfluss auf das Endergebnis. Selbst die Stufen können bei der selben Treppe alle ihre Aspekte verändern: Form, Maße, Material ...

Für die Gewährleistung der Benutzungssicherheit ist es wesentlich, dass der gesamte Verlauf der Treppe gut beleuchtet ist. Bei steilen Treppen müssen die Stufen überlappen, so dass ausreichend Auftrittfläche für den Fuß vorhanden ist. Außerdem ist zu berücksichtigen, dass überlappende Stufen auf die unteren Trittflächen Schatten werfen können und so die Sicht beeinträchtigen. Es wird daher empfohlen, die Trittstufen und Steigestufen in verschiedenen Farbtönen auszuführen oder die Ränder hervorzuheben.

Das Design der Stufen kann einen konkreten Akzent setzen. Ein gutes Beispiel dafür sind in die Wand eingebundene massive Stufen, die dem Wohnraum mehr Platz lassen. Eine andere Strategie sind Schattenkanten zwischen Treppe und Wand, wodurch die Struktur an Leichtigkeit gewinnt, oder eine nur teilweise Verkleidung oder Färbung der Stufen.

In einigen Fällen können Stufen auch neue Funktionen übernehmen: als Fläche zur Aufstellung von Dekorationsobjekten, als Teil eines Regals oder für die Unterbringung von Lichtquellen.

Dans la conception d'un escalier interviennent divers facteurs qui, combinés, peuvent aboutir à un programme varié de solutions. La situation, l'usage voire les goûts personnels influencent également le résultat final. Sur un même escalier, les marches peuvent aussi varier dans tous leurs aspects : forme, dimension, matériau…

Il est essentiel que l'escalier soit bien éclairé sur tout son parcours afin de garantir la sécurité d'usage. Quant aux escaliers compensés, les échelons doivent se chevaucher afin d'offrir une surface suffisante pour le pied. Par surcroît, il est important de tenir compte du fait que ce type de marche peut engendrer une ombre sur les échelons précédents, diminuant d'autant la visibilité. Pour ce, l'on recommande de concevoir des marches et des contre-marches avec différentes tonalités ou de marquer les bords.

Le design des marches peut aussi permettre de concrétiser une atmosphère. Un bon exemple est présenté par les marches massives encastrées dans le mur, qui libèrent une partie de la superficie pour le séjour. Une autre stratégie consiste à séparer l'escalier du mur de quelques millimètres, la structure étant alors perçue comme plus légère. Ou appliquer un revêtement ou une peinture sur une seule partie des marches.

Dans certains cas, les marches peuvent remplir une fonction indépendante. Ainsi de supports d'objets décoratifs, d'éléments intégrant une étagère ou pour accueillir des sources d'éclairage.

En el diseño de una escalera intervienen distintos factores que combinados pueden llegar a formar un variado elenco de soluciones. La ubicación, el uso y hasta las apetencias personales también influencian el resultado final. Los peldaños, asimismo, pueden variar todos sus aspectos incluso en una misma escalera: forma, dimensión, material…

Es esencial que la escalera esté bien iluminada en todo su recorrido para garantizar la seguridad de su uso. En el caso de las escaleras compensadas, los peldaños se deben solapar para proporcionar suficiente superficie para el pie. Además, se debe tener en cuenta que los peldaños solapados pueden producir sombras en las huellas inferiores, con lo que disminuiría la visibilidad. Por ello, es recomendable diseñar las huellas y contrahuellas en diferentes tonalidades o marcar los bordes.

El diseño de los peldaños puede servir a la vez para dar un aspecto concreto al ambiente. Un buen ejemplo de ello son los peldaños macizos encastados en el muro, que dejan libre mayor superficie para la estancia. Otra estrategia es separar unos milímetros la escalera de la pared, con lo que la estructura se percibe ligera, o aplicar un revestimiento o una pintura en sólo una parte de los escalones.

En algunos casos, los peldaños pueden cumplir una función independiente. Así sirven además de plataforma para colocar objetos de decoración, como elemento integrante de una estantería o para situar puntos de luz.

The dimensions, forms and materials of
steps can all be treated playfully; these
triangular steps alternate their positions, as if
they were isolated elements that had been
piled on top of each other.

Das Spiel mit Maßen, Formen und Materialien der Stufen bietet vielfältige Möglichkeiten, wie hier die dreieckigen Formen, die
versetzt angeordnet sind, als wären es
vereinzelte, aufeinandergestapelte Elemente.

Il est loisible de jouer avec les dimensions,
les formes et matériaux des échelons comme
ceux-ci : de forme triangulaire, ils font
alterner leurs positions comme s'ils figuraient
des éléments isolés ayant été empilés.

Se puede jugar con las medidas, formas y
materiales de los escalones como en estos
de forma triangular que alternan sus
posiciones como si fueran elementos
aislados que se han ido apilando.

© Roger Casas

The character of a staircase is defined by its setting and materials, as well as the curves and straight lines used in its construction.

Die geschwungenen oder geraden Linien einer Treppe, das Material und die Umgebung definieren ihren Charakter.

Les lignes, courbes ou droites, profilant un escalier, le matériau et l'environnement définissent sa personnalité.

Las líneas curvas o rectas que perfilan una escalera, el material y el entorno definen su carácter.

© Eugeni Pons

© Eugeni Pons

Handrails
Geländer
Rampes
Barandillas

For safety reasons, the building regulations for staircases in public buildings require banisters or handrails for flights of steps when they are unbounded by a wall. These regulations do not apply in family houses, but nevertheless banisters are recommended for very steep staircases, and for those that are going to be used by elderly people or children. Banisters obviously make staircases easier to use in any circumstances. Staircases used by children should have a complementary banister at a lower height – approximately 2 feet (60 cm) above the steps.

The material for a banister must be pleasant to touch, and it must be remembered that very thin or wide shapes can be difficult to grasp. Banisters can be fixed to the stairs in a number of ways, but the most common ones involve setting them directly into the steps, making them an integral part of a single structure or putting them against a wall.

The choice of material and the shape of a banister exert a great influence on the overall look of a staircase and can help to integrate it into a setting or, on the contrary, make it stand out. The form of a banister does not have to strictly follow the path of the steps but can trace curves or other shapes, designed purely on the basis of esthetic criteria. Banisters can be built in a wide variety of materials, although wood and metal are the most common. If glass is used, it must be treated to make it more secure. It is advisable to put a wooden handrail on top of a glass banister, to make it more comfortable to touch.

Für Treppen in öffentlichen Gebäuden ist aus Sicherheitsgründen für alle nicht durch eine Wand begrenzten Treppenläufe ein Geländer oder Handlauf vorgeschrieben. Für Einfamilienhäuser gelten andere Normen. Die Anbringung von Geländern empfiehlt sich bei Treppen mit ausgeprägter Neigung insbesondere für ältere Personen und Kinder; sie stellen in jedem Fall eine Hilfe dar. Treppen, die überwiegend von Kindern benutzt werden, sollten einen zusätzlichen niedrigeren Handlauf haben (etwa 60 cm ab Stufenkante).

Das Material sollte angenehm zu greifen sein, da es schwierig ist, sich an sehr schmalen oder breiten Formen festzuhalten. Unter den vielen Befestigungsarten sind die Verankerungen an den Stufen zu erwähnen, diejenigen, die Teil der Struktur sind, sowie diejenigen, die an der Mauer befestigt sind.

Die Wahl des Materials und der Form ist entscheidend für das Aussehen der Treppe und trägt dazu bei, sie in den Raum zu integrieren oder den Kontrast hervor zu heben. Die Form des Geländers muss nicht unbedingt den gesamten Verlauf der Treppenläufe begleiten, sondern kann Wendungen oder Formen gemäß ästhetischer Kriterien annehmen. Zur Herstellung steht eine große Materialvielfalt zur Verfügung, wobei Holz und Metall den ersten Platz einnehmen. Bei Ausführungen in Glas muss es sich zur Erhöhung der Sicherheit um Spezialglas handeln. Es wird empfohlen, am oberen Abschluss eines Glasgeländers einen Handlauf aus Holz anzubringen, der sich angenehmer greifen lässt.

Les normes de construction d'escaliers dans les bâtiments publics exigent des mains courantes ou des rampes pour des motifs de sécurité sur les volées non délimitées par une paroi. Ces normes ne s'appliquent pas aux logements particuliers, bien qu'elles soient recommandées pour les escaliers à forte pente ou si les usagers sont âgés ou très jeunes. Il est entendu que les mains courantes facilitent l'usage quelle que soit l'utilisation. Les escaliers destinés aux enfants devraient être équipés d'une rampe supplémentaire et plus basse (à 60 cm des marches).

Le matériau de la main courante se doit d'être agréable au toucher, les formes très fines ou très épaisses pouvant être difficiles à saisir. Coexistent nombre de types de fixations mais l'on peut noter les éléments encastrés dans les marches, ceux figurant une structure unique et ceux adossés au mur. Le choix du matériau et de la forme influence de manière la composition de l'ensemble et peuvent intégrer un escalier dans un espace ou, a contrario, le mettre en avant. La forme de la main courante ne doit pas nécessairement suivre strictement l'ensemble du parcours de l'escalier. Au contraire, elle peut dessiner courbes et formes diverses selon des critères purement esthétiques.

Bien qu'elles puissent revêtir une grande variété de matériaux, le bois et le métal prédominent. Si elles sont en verre, celui-ci doit recevoir un traitement pour assurer sa sécurité. Il est conseillé de placer une main courante de bois sur la partie supérieure des rampes de verre, pour leur conférer un toucher plus agréable.

La normativa para la construcción de escaleras en edificios públicos exige barandillas o pasamanos por razones de seguridad en los tramos no delimitados por una pared. Estas normas no se aplican en las viviendas unifamiliares, aunque se recomiendan estos elementos para escaleras muy inclinadas y si los usuarios son personas mayores y niños. Evidentemente, las barandillas facilitan el uso en cualquier utilización. Las escaleras empleadas por niños deberían tener una barandilla complementaria a menor altura (aproximadamente a unos 60 cm de los peldaños).

El material para la barandilla ha de ser agradable al tacto, ya que las formas muy finas o muy gruesas pueden ser difíciles de agarrar. Las maneras de fijación son numerosas, pero destacan los elementos que se encastan en los peldaños, los que forman parte de una única estructura y los adosados al muro.

La elección del material y de la forma tiene gran influencia en la composición del conjunto y puede ayudar a integrar la escalera en el espacio o por el contrario resaltarla. La forma de la barandilla no tiene que seguir estrictamente el recorrido de los tramos en todo su desarrollo, sino que puede dibujar curvas u otras formas que se diseñan siguiendo criterios estéticos.

Se pueden construir de una gran variedad de materiales, aunque prevalecen la madera y el metal. Si se realizan en vidrio este debe estar tratado para aumentar su seguridad. Se aconseja colocar un pasamanos de madera en la parte superior de las barandillas de vidrio, para hacerlas más agradables al tacto.

In former times the staircases of important buildings were designed and created by fully-fledged artists and craftsmen; the results are breathtakingly impressive.

In vergangenen Jahrhunderten entwarfen und schufen wahre Künstler und Handwerker die Geländer repräsentativer Gebäude; die Ergebnisse vermitteln eine eindrucksvolle Erhabenheit.

Au cours des siècles passés, les mains-courantes des bâtiments les plus éminents furent conçues et créées par de véritables artistes et artisans avec comme résultat une majesté grandiose.

En siglos pasados las barandillas de edificios representativos fueron diseñadas y creados por verdaderos artistas y artesanos; el resultado es de una majestuosidad impresionante.

Metal banisters offer infinite design possibilities: an elegant curve can be traced with a slither of stainless steel, or a metal cable can be stretched on a wooden frame as a safety feature alongside a flight of stairs.

Metallgeländer bieten unendliche Designmöglichkeiten: z. B. kann mit einem Minimum an Edelstahl ein eleganter Schwung erreicht oder durch ein in einen Holzrahmen eingespanntes Metallkabel ein Treppenlauf seitlich abgesichert werden.

Les rampes métalliques offrent une infinité de design : une courbe élégante peut, ainsi, être tracée avec un minimum d'acier inox, ou un câble métallique être tendu dans un cadre en bois pour assurer latéralement une volée.

Las barandillas metálicas ofrecen una infinidad de diseños: p. ej. se puede trazar una elegante curva con un mínimo de acero inoxidable o tensar un cable metálico en un marco de madera para asegurar el lateral de un tramo.

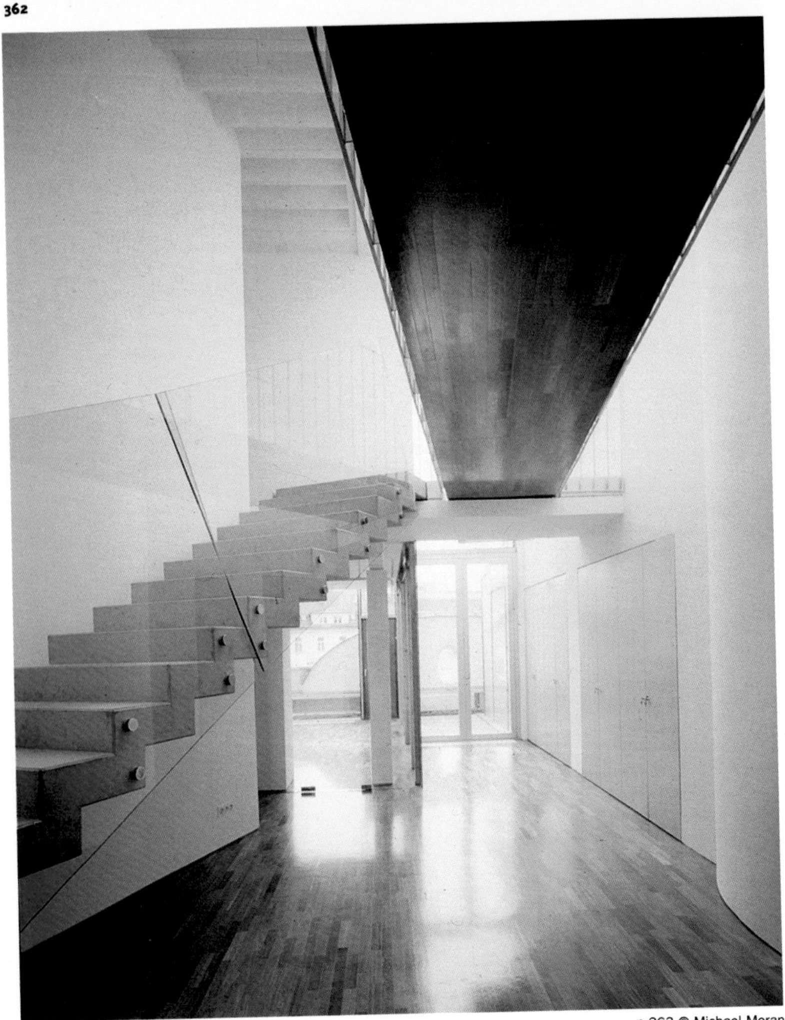

© Margherita Spiluttini

p.363 © Michael Moran

The form of a banister does not have to follow the straight or zigzagging outlines of the staircase. A small deviation can prove highly original, without detracting from the functionality.

Die Form des Geländers muss nicht unbedingt der zickzackförmigen oder geradlinigen Silhouette der Treppe folgen. Eine kleine Abweichung kann sehr originell wirken, ohne die Funktionalität zu beeinträchtigen.

La forme de la main courante n'épouse pas nécessairement la silhouette, en zigzag ou rectiligne, de l'escalier. Une légère déviation peut imprimer une touche d'originalité sans retirer la fonctionnalité.

La forma de la barandilla no necesariamente sigue la silueta zigzagueante o rectilínea de la escalera. Un pequeño 'desvío' puede resultar muy original sin restarle funcionalidad.

© Norbert Miguletz (2 photos)

Illumination
Beleuchtung
Illumination
Iluminación

The lighting on staircases has to be considered in depth as it plays a crucial role in making steps safe to use. It is the best to opt for lighting that remains constant from one end of the staircase to the other.

The insertion of a skylight over the top of a stairwell can be a good solution, as sunlight will illuminate the whole staircase to an equal degree. In cases where the staircase has no direct access to the roof, another option is to open up holes – of any shape or size – in the side walls or at the top and bottom of the staircase. Artificial lighting can be either direct or indirect; the latter is preferable, however, as it does not cast any strong shadows on the treads. The steps of a compensated staircase overlap and the upper steps throw shadows on those below, so lamps must be installed parallel with the flights and only a short distance above them. If it is decided to hang lamps directly above the steps, they must be sufficiently high to allow for the passage of large objects up and down the stairs.

Lighting can totally transform the look of a staircase by focusing on its most significant features and design details, or by emphasizing the finish of the materials used in its construction.

Die Beleuchtung der Treppen muss sorgfältig durchdacht werden, weil davon größtenteils deren Sicherheit abhängt. Der gesamte Verlauf der Treppen muss gleichmäßig beleuchtet werden.

Eine gute Lösung dafür ist ein Oberlicht über dem Treppenschacht, da das natürliche Licht den ganzen Verlauf gleichmäßig erhellt. Wenn die Verbindung zum Dach nicht direkt ist, müssen Öffnungen – jeglicher Form und Größe – in den seitlichen Mauern oder an den Enden der Treppe geschaffen werden.

Die künstliche Beleuchtung kann direkt oder indirekt erfolgen, wobei letztere vorzuziehen ist, da hierdurch keine Schatten auf die Stufen geworfen werden. Bei einer sehr steilen Treppe überlappen sich die Stufen und es entstehen Schatten auf den darunterliegenden Trittflächen; die Lichtquellen sollten daher parallel zu den Treppenläufen und in geringer Höhe angebracht werden. Wenn man sich für Hängelampen über den Treppenläufen entscheidet, muss eine ausreichende Höhe berücksichtigt und daran gedacht werden, dass man auch mit Lasten ungehindert hinauf- und hinuntersteigen kann.

Eine durchdachte Beleuchtung kann das Aussehen einer Treppe vollkommen verändern: durch das Hervorheben wesentlicher Elemente, von Details oder der Betonung der Oberflächenbehandlung der Materialien, die zu ihrer Konstruktion verwendet wurden.

L'éclairage des escaliers doit être pensé avec soin, sa sécurité d'utilisation en dépendant pour une partie non négligeable. L'ensemble du parcours doit être illuminé de façon homogène.

Une claire-voie située en haut du regard de l'escalier constitue une bonne solution, la lumière naturelle pouvant se diffuser harmonieusement. En l'absence de relation directe avec la couverte, il faut opter pour des ouvertures – de toutes formes et tailles – dans les parois latérales ou aux extrémités de l'escalier.

Un éclairage artificiel peut être direct ou indirect, cette dernière option étant à privilégier puisqu'elle ne produit pas d'ombres prononcées sur les marches. Un escalier compensé voit ses marches se chevaucher et naître des ombres sur les échelons inférieurs. De ce fait les lampes devraient être positionnées parallèlement aux volées et à faible hauteur. Dans l'éventualité de lumière surplombant les escaliers, il est nécessaire de respecter une hauteur suffisante, en gardant à l'esprit la montée et la descente avec des charges.

L'éclairage peut complètement modifier l'aspect d'un escalier, soulignant ses parties les plus significatives et ses détails ou mettant en avant la finition de ses matériaux de construction.

L a iluminación de las escaleras se tiene que pensar detalladamente ya que la seguridad de su uso depende en buena parte de ello. Se ha de tender a iluminar de manera homogénea todo el recorrido.

La ubicación de una claraboya en lo alto del hueco de la escalera es una buena solución, ya que la luz natural baña todo el desarrollo por igual. Cuando la relación con la cubierta no es directa, se debe optar por abrir huecos –de cualquier forma y tamaño– en los muros laterales o en los extremos de la escalera.

La iluminación artificial puede ser directa o indirecta; aunque esta última es preferible, ya que no produce sombras pronunciadas en los peldaños. En una escalera compensada los escalones se solapan y se originan sombras en las huellas inferiores por lo que la instalación de lámparas debería ser paralela a los tramos y a poca altura de estos. Si se opta por colgar fuentes de luz encima de los tramos, se debe respetar una altura suficiente, teniendo en cuenta también la subida o bajada con carga.

La iluminación puede cambiar totalmente el aspecto de una escalera, resaltando sus partes más significativas, los detalles constructivos o enfatizando el acabado de los materiales con los que se ha levantado.

The carefully calculated artificial lighting of this minimalist staircase takes on a starring role at nightfall.

Durch die durchdachte künstliche Beleuchtung spielt diese minimalistische Treppe nachts eindeutig die Hauptrolle.

De nuit, un éclairage artificiel étudié offre le premier rôle à cet escalier minimaliste.

Con una estudiada iluminación artificial esta escalera minimalista se convierte en el claro protagonista durante la noche.

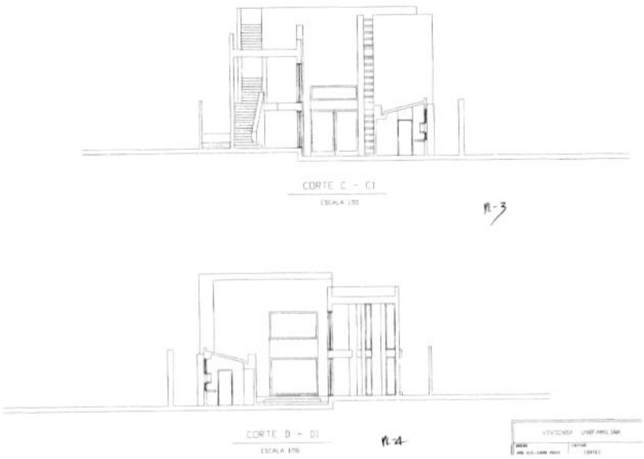

Strategically spaced doors or windows and meticulous lighting of the steps are essential for ensuring that a staircase is safe; they also emphasize the design features.

Jede Art strategisch angebrachter Tür- oder Fensteröffnungen und die sorgfältige Beleuchtung der Stufen sind wesentlich für die Gewährleistung der Sicherheit der Treppen und unterstreichen außerdem ihr Design.

CORTE C - C'
ESCALA 1:50

fi 3

CORTE B - B'
ESCALA 1:50

fi 4

© Chris Gascoigne/View

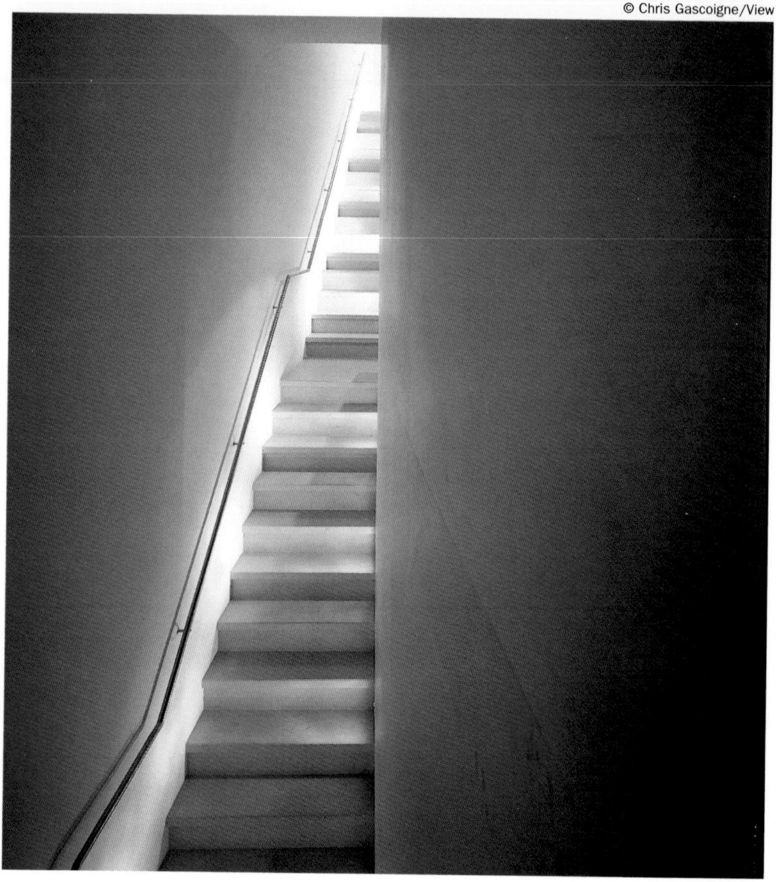

Les ouvertures en tout genre, disposées stratégiquement, et un éclairage minutieux des marches sont essentiels pour garantir la sécurité des escaliers. Par surcroît, ils mettent en valeur le design de l'escalier.

Las aperturas de todo tipo estratégicamente colocadas y la cuidadosa iluminación de escalones son esenciales para garantizar la seguridad de las escaleras; Además, subrayan el diseño de la escalera.

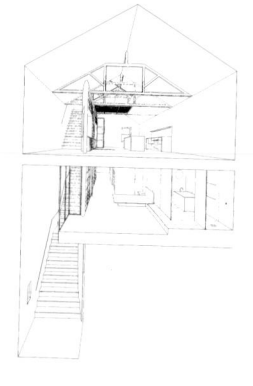

© Eugeni Pons (2 photos)

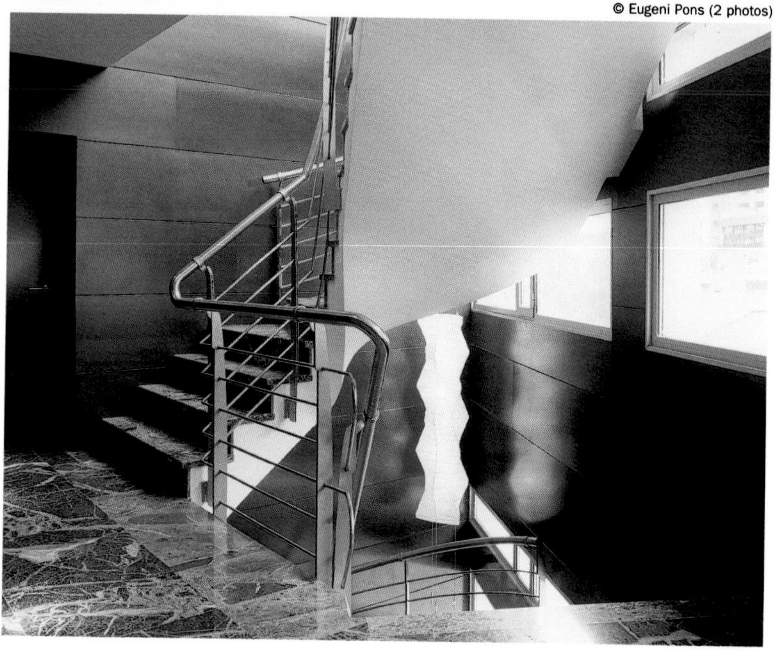

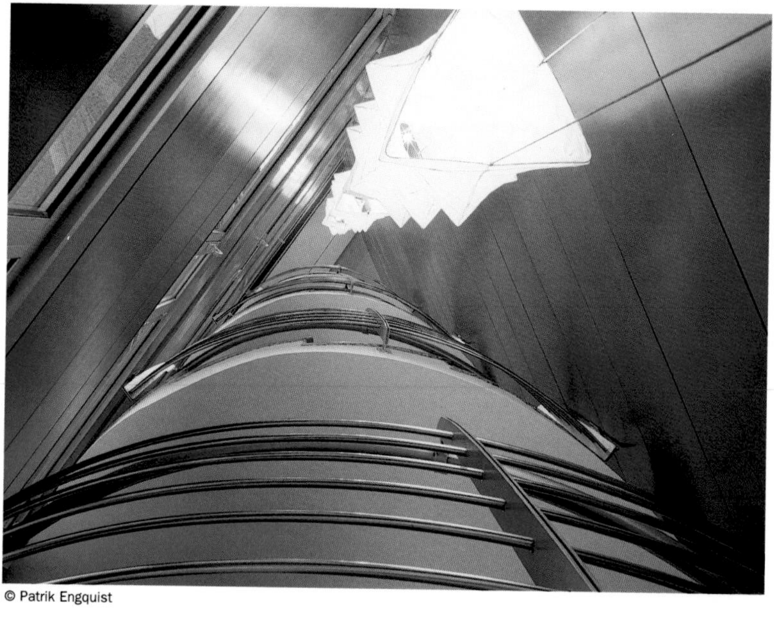

© Patrik Engquist

Double use
Zweifacher Nutzen
Double usage
Doble uso

A staircase is built to bridge a gap between different levels. However, it is also undoubtedly an element that can bestow character on a space and exert a crucial influence on its overall appearance. Moreover, the structure of a staircase can also be put to other uses, to become, for example, an integral part of a bookcase, or a support for a lamp. Minor modifications can transform a stairwell into a closet or even a small room.

A staircase is sometimes built, over and above its strict functional purpose, as a nerve center around which the other rooms are organized. Its strong compositional features can turn it into a building's dominant feature.

One option in confined spaces is the use of movable or folding staircases, which can be kept out of sight when they are not needed. These are usually made of metal or wood, as these are light materials that are easy to handle. Another space-saving variation consists of a steep, narrow staircase with steps that are cut off in the middle on alternate sides, so that either the right or the left foot always has to lead when going up or coming down. It is not advisable to use such staircases for carrying heavy loads; it is also a good idea to add banisters, to make them easier to use, although even so they are out of the question for spaces which are used intensively, or for people with problems of mobility.

E ine Treppe dient zur Überwindung von Höhen verschiedener Ebenen. Zweifellos ist sie auch ein Element, das einem Raum Persönlichkeit verleiht und bestimmend seine Ästhetik beeinflusst. Ihre Struktur kann aber auch anderen Zwecken dienen: als Bestandteil eines Regals oder zur Unterbringung einer Lichtquelle. Mit Hilfe kleiner Änderungen kann der Treppenschacht in einen Schrank oder sogar in ein kleines Zimmer umgewandelt werden.

Abgesehen von ihrer unbestreitbaren Funktionalität wird eine Treppe gelegentlich zu einem zentralen Kern, um den sich die Räume gruppieren. Ihre kompositorische Kraft kann sie zu einem einzigartigen Element des Gebäudes machen.

Auf engem Raum kann man sich für Zug- oder Falttreppen entscheiden, die nach Gebrauch weggeklappt werden können. Sie sind normalerweise aus Metall oder Holz, da diese Materialien leicht und einfach zu handhaben sind. Eine weitere Variante zur Platzersparnis sind Raumspartreppen, die sehr steil sind und bei denen man den Aufstieg oder Abstieg immer mit dem rechten oder linken Fuß beginnen muss. Für die Beförderung von Lasten sind sie nicht zu empfehlen. Es sollten hier Geländer angebracht werden, um die Benutzung zu erleichtern. Sie sind daher für häufige Nutzung oder für Menschen mit eingeschränkter Bewegungsfähigkeit nicht empfohlen.

Un escalier a pour objet de permettre de franchir des niveaux. Cependant, il s'agit également d'un élément susceptible de conférer une personnalité à un espace, influant de manière déterminante sur son esthétique. Sa structure peut, par ailleurs, être détournée de son usage premier. Comme partie intégrante d'une étagère ou pour accueillir une source de lumière. De légères modifications peuvent convertir l'espace inutilisé sous l'escalier en armoire, voire en petite pièce.

Hormis sa stricte fonctionnalité, l'escalier peut parfois s'ériger en élément névralgique, autour duquel se distribuent les pièces. Sa force de composition peut le métamorphoser en l'élément clé de la construction.

Dans les espaces confinés, il est loisible d'opter pour des escaliers escamotables ou pliables, pouvant disparaître lorsqu'ils ne sont pas employés. Ils sont habituellement en métal ou en bois, la légèreté de ces matériaux les rendant plus facilement manipulables. Les escaliers aux marches décalées constituent une autre voie pour économiser l'espace. Leur inclinaison prononcée implique de commencer la montée ou la descente toujours avec le même pied, gauche ou droit. Ils ne sont pas recommandés pour déplacer des charges. Les mains courantes, pratiques, sont vivement conseillées pour cet usage. Ils sont, de ce fait, à éviter pour les lieux d'affluence ou pour les usagers à mobilité limitée.

Una escalera se construye para salvar las alturas entre diferentes niveles. Indudablemente, es también un elemento que puede conferir carácter a un espacio, influyendo de forma determinante en su estética. Su estructura, además, puede servir para otros usos: como parte integrante de una estantería o para instalar una fuente de luz. Mediante pequeñas modificaciones, se puede convertir el hueco de la escalera en un armario, e incluso en una pequeña habitación.

Aparte de su estricta funcionalidad, la escalera se erige en ocasiones como un elemento neurálgico, alrededor del cual se organizan las estancias. Su fuerza compositiva puede convertirlas en el elemento singular de la edificación.

En espacios reducidos se puede optar por escaleras levadizas o plegables, que se pueden esconder cuando no se necesitan. Acostumbran a ser metálicas o de madera, ya que estos materiales son ligeros y pueden manipularse fácilmente. Otra variante para ahorrar espacio son las escaleras con peldaños desfasados, que tienen una pronunciada inclinación en las cuales la subida o bajada siempre se tiene que iniciar con el pie derecho o izquierdo. No se recomienda utilizarlas para desplazar cargas. Es conveniente la colocación de barandillas, que facilitan su uso. Por todo ello, no son recomendables en espacios transitados, ni para usuarios con dificultades de movilidad.

© Jordi Miralles
p. 388-389 © Jordi Miralles (2 photos)

© Hiroyuki Hirai (2 photos)

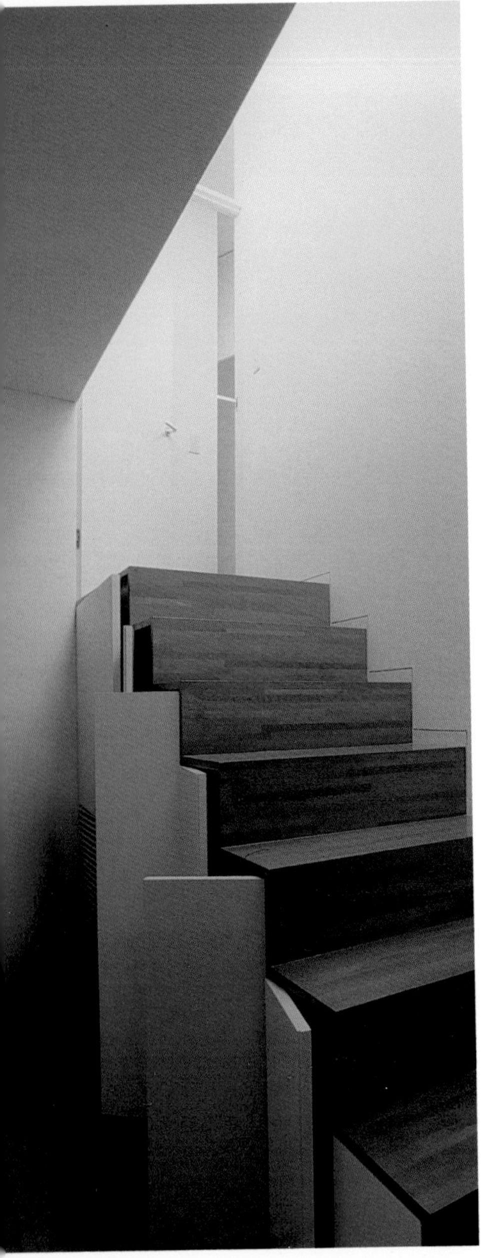

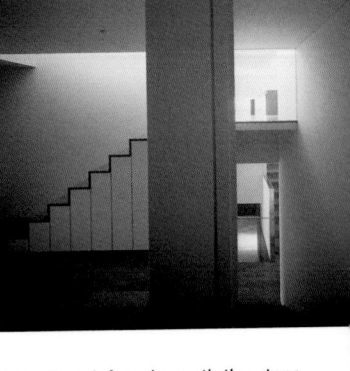

The space left underneath the steps can be exploited to create storage spaces in the form of open shelves, closets with doors, drawers... or to install a decorative element, such as a lamp.

Der sich unter den Läufen ergebende Platz kann für die Schaffung von Stauraum in Form von offenen Regalen, Schränken mit geschlossenen Türen, Schubladen etc... oder für den Einbau von Elementen, z. B. einer Lichtquelle, verwendet werden.

L'espace né sous les volées peut être mis à profit en créant des espaces de rangement sous la forme d'étagères ouvertes, d'armoires fermées par des portes, de tiroirs...ou pour insérer un nouvel élément, telle une source de lumière.

El espacio resultante debajo de los tramos se puede aprovechar creando espacios de almacenaje en forma de estanterías abiertas, armarios cerrados con puertas, cajones... o para colocar cualquier elemento como p. ej. una fuente de luz.

© Eduard Hueber

© Luis Asín (2 photos)

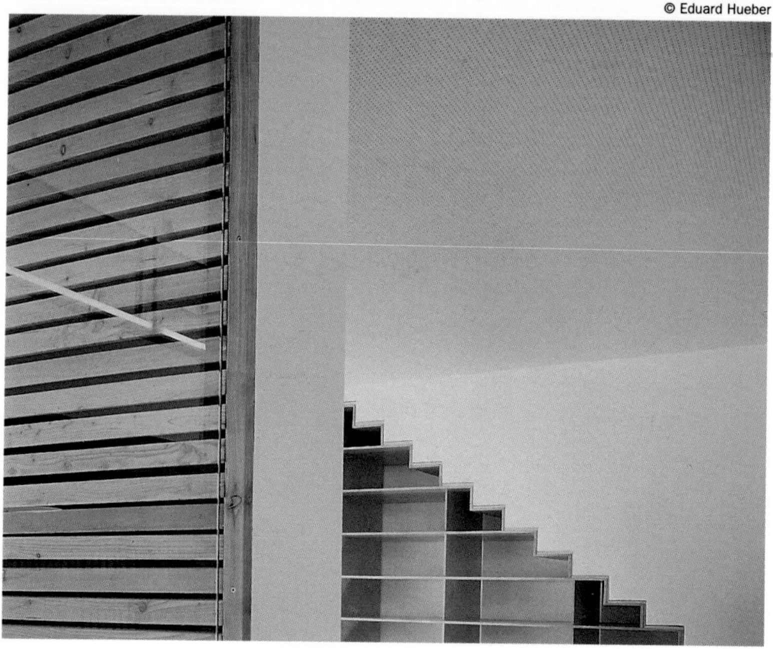

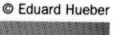

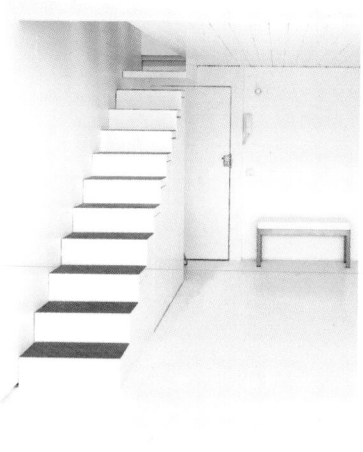

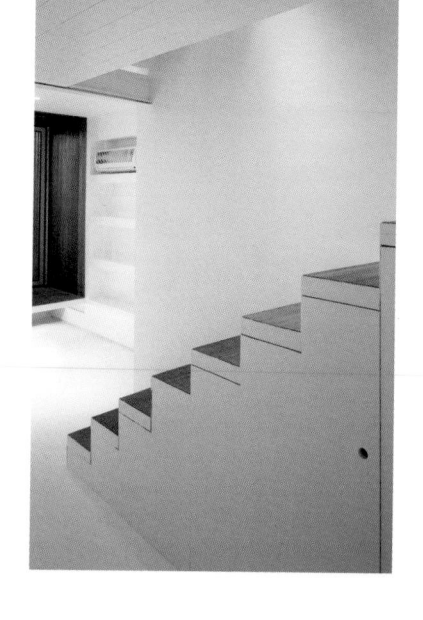

© Andrea Martiradonna (3 photos)

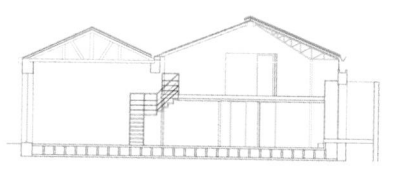

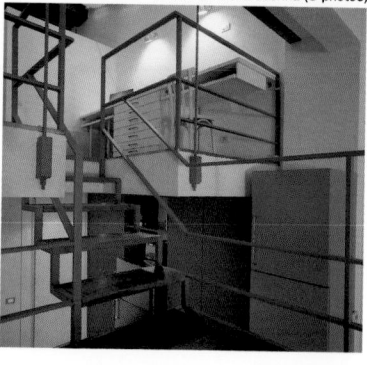

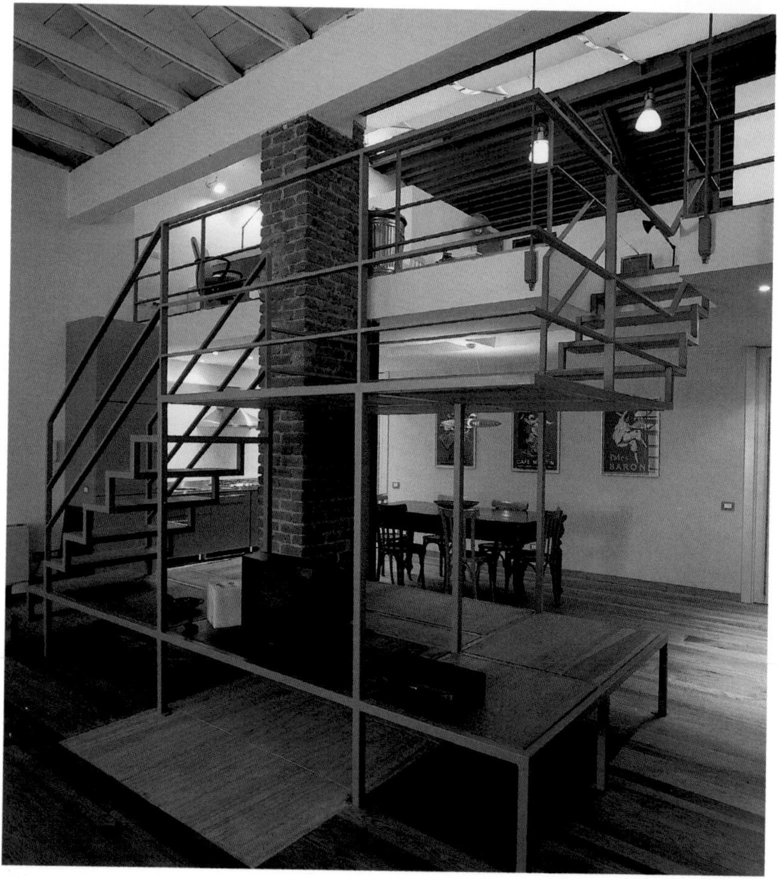

© Zona 5 (2 photos)

© Koji Kobayashi & Nobuaki Nakagawa

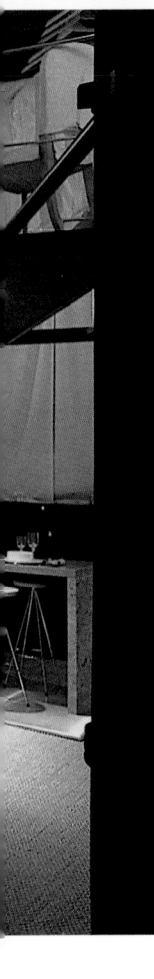

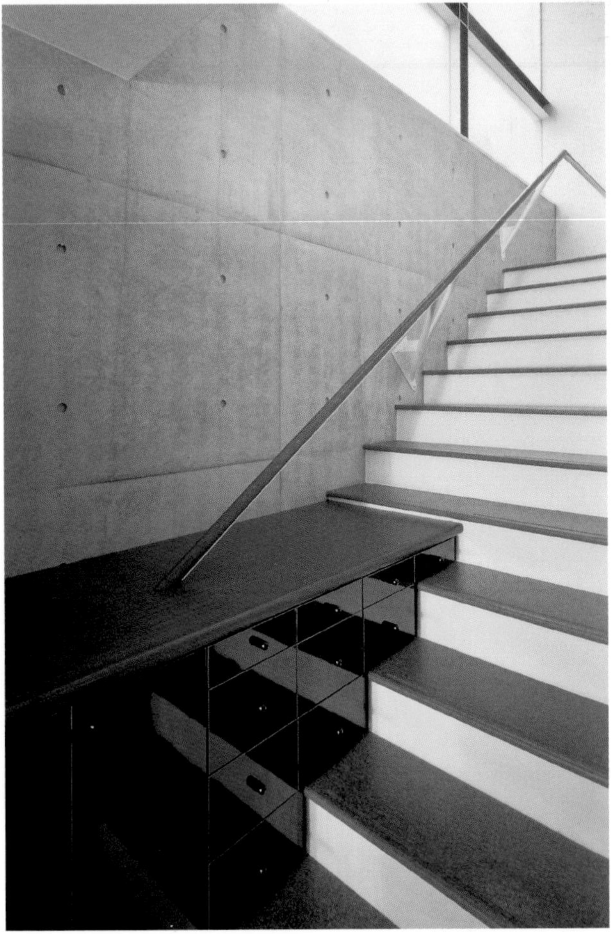

Storage space can even be found under a sharply compensated staircase – and, what is more, it can also prove highly decorative.

Sogar unter einer Raumspartreppe kann man Platz für Regale gewinnen, der außerdem noch sehr dekorativ wirkt.

Même sous un escalier très compensé il est possible de gagner de l'espace de rangement qui, en outre, se révèlera très décoratif.

Incluso debajo de una escalera muy compensada se puede ganar espacio de almacenaje que, además, resulta muy decorativo.